DATE DUE

Demco, Inc. 38-293

CARLOS SANTANA

Recent Titles in Greenwood Biographies

CARLOS SANTANA

A Biography

Norman Weinstein

GREENWOOD BIOGRAPHIES

GREENWOOD PRESS
An Imprint of ABC-CLIO, LLC

A B C 🦅 C L I O

Santa Barbara, California • Denver, Colorado • Oxford, England

Library of Congress Cataloging-in-Publication Data

Weinstein, Norman, 1948–
    Carlos Santana : a biography / Norman Weinstein.
        p. cm.—(Greenwood biographies)
    Includes discography (p.), bibliographical references (p.), and index.
    ISBN 978-0-313-35420-5 (hard copy : alk. paper)—ISBN 978-0-313-35421-2 (ebook)
    1. Santana, Carlos. 2. Rock musicians—United States—Biography. I. Title.
ML419.S22W45   2009
787.87′164092—dc22
[B]   2009019683

13 12 11 10 09   1 2 3 4 5

This book is also available on the World Wide Web as an eBook.
Visit www.abc-clio.com for details.

ABC-CLIO, LLC
130 Cremona Drive, P.O. Box 1911
Santa Barbara, California 93116-1911

This book is printed on acid-free paper ∞

Manufactured in the United States of America

CONTENTS

Photo essay follows page 56

SERIES FOREWORD

In response to high school and public library needs, Greenwood developed this distinguished series of full-length biographies specifically for student use. Prepared by field experts and professionals, these engaging biographies are tailored for high school students who need challenging yet accessible biographies. Ideal for secondary school assignments, the length, format, and subject areas are designed to meet educators' requirements and students' interests.

Greenwood offers an extensive selection of biographies spanning all curriculum-related subject areas including social studies, the sciences, literature and the arts, history and politics, as well as popular culture, covering public figures and famous personalities from all time periods and backgrounds, both historic and contemporary, who have made an impact on American and/or world culture. Greenwood biographies were chosen based on comprehensive feedback from librarians and educators. Consideration was given to both curriculum relevance and inherent interest. The result is an intriguing mix of the well known and the unexpected, the saints and sinners from long-ago history and contemporary pop culture. Readers will find a wide array of subject choices from fascinating crime figures like Al Capone to inspiring pioneers like Margaret Mead, from the greatest minds of our time like Stephen Hawking to the most amazing success stories of our day like J. K. Rowling.

While the emphasis is on fact, not glorification, the books are meant to be fun to read. Each volume provides in-depth information about the subject's life from birth through childhood, the teen years, and adulthood. A thorough account relates family background and education, traces personal and professional influences, and explores struggles, accomplishments, and contributions. A timeline highlights the most significant life events against a historical perspective. Bibliographies supplement the reference value of each volume.

ACKNOWLEDGMENTS

Books are team efforts. I would like to express appreciation to
Therese Boyd, my sharply perceptive copyeditor, Bob DiForio, my lit-
erary agent; Kristi Ward and George Butler, who helped move this
book along the road to publication; my correspondents about music
and culture, Professors Robert Farris Thompson and John Szwed at
Yale University; Dr. Ken Bilby at the Center for Black Music
Research at Columbia College, Chicago; music critic Gary Giddins;
and independent scholar Morton Marks. And to my beloved Mary,
my wife and most inspiring artistic and intellectual companion, with
whom every day is music.

TIMELINE: EVENTS IN THE LIFE OF CARLOS SANTANA

1947	Carlos Santana is born to Jose Santana and Josefina Barragan in Autlan de Navarro, Mexico.
1952	Receives first lessons in reading music and playing violin, accompanying his father in public concerts of mariachi music.
1960	Abandons the violin and begins electric guitar lessons, driven by blues he hears on U.S. radio. First professional gig is at El Convoy, a run-down Tijuana bar.
1963	Moves to San Francisco. Attends Mission High School, where he excels at art, but mainly goes to concerts at the Fillmore to see artists such as B. B. King and Jimi Hendrix perform.
1966	Performs for the first time with nationally recognized rock musicians during a jam at the Fillmore. Founds first group, the Santana Blues Band.
1967	The Santana Blues Band opens for The Who.
1968	Records his first guitar tracks for *The Live Adventures of Mike Bloomfield and Al Kooper* (released by Columbia Records, 1969).
1969	With his band now known as Santana, performs to an enthusiastic audience of a half-million at the Woodstock Music Festival. Leads to a recording contract with Columbia Records and first album.

1970   The Santana band starts work on the next album, *Abraxas*, which includes "Black Magic Woman" and the salsa classic "Oye Como Va." *Abraxas* becomes one of the top 50 best-selling albums of the year.

1971   Recording sessions for the final album for the original Santana band, *Santana III*, showcases the interplay between Carlos and the new second guitarist, Neal Schon. The sessions are marred by in-fighting in the band.

1972   Changes name to "Devadip Carlos Santana," making public his spiritual allegiance to the Indian guru Sri Chinmoy. The new Santana band records the jazz-infused *Caravanserai* album.

1973   Marries Deborah King, daughter of R&B guitarist Saunders King. The new Santana band records two watershed albums, *Welcome* and *Lotus*, crystallizing the band's new jazz-rock synthesis practiced during a world concert tour. Jazz vocalist Leon Thomas becomes the first of several musicians identified with the jazz avant-garde revolution of the 1960s spearheaded by John Coltrane to collaborate with Carlos.

1977   A double-album culled from studio sessions and live concerts, *Moonflower*, receives the most international commercial acceptance since *Santana III*. The album signals a return to more Latin rock, less jazz.

1981   With wife Deborah, severs connection to guru Sri Chinmoy, marking the beginning of a new commitment to Christianity and New Age mysticism.

1983   Son Salvador is born. Two daughters, Stella and Angelica, would complete their family by 1990.

1989   The most jazz-flavored and instrumental-driven album of the 1980s, *Blues for Salvador*, wins a Grammy for Best Rock Instrumental.

1991   Terminates his 22-year-old association with Columbia Records over marketing strategies and signs with Polydor Records. Three deaths—promoter Bill Graham, Stevie Ray Vaughan, and Miles Davis—deeply impact Carlos.

1995   In psychotherapy, discovers that sexual molestation he suffered as a child from an American tourist in Tijuana left him with lingering psychological problems and dedicates himself to overcoming those problems.

1998   With wife Deborah, establishes the Milagro Foundation to help children in need internationally.

1999   Signs with Arista Records run by old business colleague
         Clive Davis and records *Supernatural*, the most commer-
         cially successful album of his career, selling over 25 million
         copies. It wins eight Grammys and links Carlos to emergent
         younger artists.

2004   The Latin wing of the National Academy of Recordings
         Arts and Sciences honors Carlos with the "Person of the
         Year" award.

2005   Finds himself at the center of political controversy because
         he wore a t-shirt with Che Guevara's portrait to the Acad-
         emy Awards. Cuban exiles call for protests at Santana con-
         certs and the boycotting of his albums. Controversy spreads
         when he appears as a guest artist on an album by the staunch
         anti-Communist, Cuban American vocalist Gloria Estefan.

2008   Wife Deborah files for divorce. Carlos launches into a new
         musical direction with the help of producer Bill Laswell.
         Appears in concert as the opener for his son's band. Also
         lends his energies to establishing a national holiday in
         honor of Cesar Chavez.

Chapter 1

IT'S A SANTANA FAMILY AFFAIR

It is impossible to hear a single guitar note played by Carlos Santana and not recognize that it is his sound. It is the "cry" he coaxes from his electric guitar, loved by millions of fans globally. And while the word "cry" might evoke sadness, the cry that Santana plays is more often ecstatically joyful. It is not the guitar sound of the Beatles' song "While My Guitar Gently Weeps." It is the cry of a guitar soaring beyond old musical horizons in search of the meaning of life through music. That might sound like serious business—and it is for Carlos Santana. But he has also created pop music just for fun, for carnivals and international music festivals, even for weddings and charitable fundraising events, in cities on every continent. The conflict between his identities as a serious rock music experimenter versus the fun-driven, popular, mainstream rock guitar wizard provoking a crowd to dance may never be settled. In fact, music lovers may be richer because of his two competing musical identities. Like the contemporary jazz-fusion guitarist Pat Metheny, being two-sided as a musician does not have to be a schizophrenic endeavor. The more commercial and pop-colored side of a musician's personality can productively coexist with the experimental side, although Carlos and Metheny are among an elite handful of musicians who have been successful working in both camps.

TRACING THE SANTANA FAMILY'S MUSICAL HERITAGE

To understand the complex and brilliant musician Carlos Santana, look deeply into his Mexican family roots. There were two generations of professional musicians in the Santana family when Carlos was born on July 20, 1947, in the tiny Mexican village of Autlán. Although it took Carlos many years to fully accept his musical connection with his family, a heritage spanning generations, he certainly strongly felt the direct impact of his father, José, who was also his first music teacher and bandleader. When Carlos was five, José began to teach him violin, as José had been taught by his father. Antonino, Carlos's grandfather, was a French horn player in a local band who struggled to make a living through music in the Mexican town of Cuautla. Perhaps aware than a violinist might have a better chance than a French horn player at making a decent living by playing in cafés and dance halls, Antonino taught José the violin.[1] The economical instability following World War I in rural Mexico made the future job prospects for a local musician seem slight. But José had a passion for music from a young age. The lessons that José learned from his father, and would pass on to Carlos, included the following:

A freelance professional musician has to be willing to perform a wide variety of musical styles (folk, classical, and pop) in order to please a wide spectrum of audiences.

All musical styles are worthy of equal respect since all music is tied to people's need for emotional, heartfelt expression through memorable melodies.

In order to make a living, a musician has to travel to where the jobs are and not be fixated on trying to earn an income from home.

The point about a musician having to move around in order to make a living José learned at a young age when his family moved from Cuautla in southern Mexico to Autlán in the northwest. José came into personal and professional maturity in Autlán. Apart from an impressive Catholic church established by missionaries in the late sixteenth century, the town of Autlán seemed securely locked in a mundane agricultural way of life. Modern amenities like electricity and indoor plumbing were largely missing. The most common occupation for the few thousand residents was farming, specifically raising corn and wheat, and raising livestock. It might have seemed an odd choice of residence for a professional musician, apart from the opportunity to play music at the church, which José did often. But the provincialism of Autlán allowed José to feel like "a big fish in a small pond." He had a starring role in the musical events celebrating life's turning points—and Autlán proved a convenient hub for traveling for gigs through Mexico and the United States. Most centrally, it was there he discovered Josefina Barragan as his partner for life. They married in 1940.

José and Josefina Santana created a large family, including three boys, Antonio, Carlos, and Jorge, and four girls, Louise, Irma, Lelicia, and Maria. Supporting this large a family in a rural village where agriculture was the main occupation was daunting to José. But he remembered his father's lessons concerning the importance of performing a wide variety of musical styles in order to satisfy the largest possible range of listeners and dancers. By creating a band, Los Cardinales, which played dance-inducing, jazzy versions of folk and pop melodies, José offered his listeners spirited and upbeat music to help them endure times of economic and political uncertainty. His repertoire included traditional Mexican popular melodies as well as versions of Duke Ellington's and Cole Porter's songs.[2]

The Santanas lived in northwestern Mexico within range of American radio programming. Captured through the radio, big band jazz, urban music, and Cole Porter's urbane songs could be appropriated by rural musicians interested in treating their audiences to the latest musical trends. Granted, to transfer the enormously dense, multilayered sound of an American jazz band into a small ensemble where acoustic guitars and violin were lead instruments took some doing. Ellington's and Porter's tunes were simplified and presented as catchy melodies more than platforms for extended improvisations. But even adjusting American jazz to Mexican rural taste, musical trends come and go quickly everywhere, and by the time Carlos had his first musical lesson from his father in 1952, Mexican listeners were less absorbed by the jazzy swing of the prewar era and more enamored of melodic music rooted in Mexican folk traditions. Carlos recalled his earliest music lessons from his father in an interview with music journalist Steve Heilig:

> In Autlán he taught me how to read [music] when I was very young. And he taught me the violin in Tijuana, and he would drill me on it, on all sorts of European music. After a while I started going out on the street with two other guys with guitars, and it was like, "Song, mister? Fifty cents." We played all the stereotypic Mexican songs.[3]

The reference Carlos made to "European" music referred to "European classical." In fact, one of the earliest violin pieces he learned was by Beethoven. This might sound odd in the context of growing up in rural Mexico where live symphony orchestra concerts were not available, but the belief that professional Mexican musicians had in a foundation of "the classics" was part of the Mexican legacy of once having been a Spanish colony. Spanish children interested in music had to rehearse their three B's—Bach, Beethoven, and Brahms—and Carlos, along with other Mexican children of the 1950s, had the same musical curriculum.

As Carlos related to Steve Heilig, the lofty world of the European classical masters soon gave way to performing "stereotypic Mexican songs." This meant for Carlos performing the style his father José was performing in the 1950s. Mariachi music was then enshrined as the national music of Mexico and was the soundtrack to all celebrations, informal at the village level to most formal at the inauguration of a new president in Mexico City.

José Santana switched gears quickly from his jazzy pop sounds and became an accomplished violinist in a traveling mariachi band. Mariachi is based on folk tunes likely inherited from Spain and has been played for decades on acoustic instruments, grouped in pairs, consisting of Spanish acoustic guitar, violin, trumpets, an acoustic bass, and hand-held percussion, usually maracas. Traditionally, a single male vocalist sings a romantic lyric. A common topic is pleading for love, a Mexican variation on the universal theme of "Do not forsake me, oh my darling." In public, these sounds were meant to enliven social interactions among all ages and generations and spark dancing. In private, the tunes were used to woo a beloved, something José Santana did to woo Josefina. It is romantic music still played to mark rites of passage, peppering family events like births, school graduations, and weddings. There is also an element of mariachi music that reinforced a certain American stereotype of the Mexican peasant: colorful, exotic adorned in serape with sombrero, romantic, and somewhat more "primitive" and earthy in music and romance supposedly than Americans.

Before he became a teenager, Carlos played "second fiddle" in his father's band. A poignant photograph of Carlos at age 10 with his father and the members of his father's mariachi band was displayed publicly for the first time in the "American Sabor" show at the Experience Music Project museum in Seattle in 2007.[4] The young Carlos appears in the photograph rather ill at ease, stiffly holding his violin that he never identified with musically. He was bored with mariachi music as well as with the violin, and dreamt of playing guitar for bands like he heard on radio broadcasts during the early days of rock. Mariachi music is a rigidly structured, formal music that should be played conventionally within a strict form. It is not music that invites musicians to radically explore or freely express their emotions, unless they are rare masters whose moments of inspiration would occasionally be welcomed. Carlos wanted to express a lot of deep feelings musically, the peaks and vales of an ambitious young man wanting to carve out a better life for himself through self-expression, so he wanted to improvise on his violin, something his father had little patience for. Angry words were often exchanged between father and son. Those acrimonious encounters happened often apparently since Carlos remarked years later that as a child he had played "stereotypic Mexican music":

> [A]nd I was like, "I hate this stuff," and had started listening to Muddy Waters, Jimmy Reed, John Lee Hooker.... Blues was my first love, yeah.... From then I started rebelling. I found myself in the shantytown, where it smells like piss and puke ... and I was there playing with my dad.... And I'm watching all this as a kid, thinking, "Damn, this planet is funky." And my father looks at me and says, "What's the matter with you?" Because I didn't look like I was having fun, and I said, "Man, I don't wanna be here. I don't want to live in this kind of scene."[5]

FAMILY PUSH-PULLS

The rebellious feelings Carlos felt in that shantytown bar kept growing. Yet, like all stories of teenage rebellion against parental authority, the story had sudden and unexpected twists and turns. His father was not present in the Santana household for long periods of time when Carlos was a boy, for both legitimate and dubious reasons. José Santana spent over a year at a time away from the family home, a separation caused, according to his repeated explanations to Josefina, by his need to travel in order to make a living. But the family theme of "absent dad due to finances" was ruptured in 1955. José had been away from home for an unusually long time. Distrustful of his explanations and suspecting that her husband was cheating on her, Josefina gathered her children up for an epic taxi ride from Autlán to Tijuana, where the family discovered José living with another woman.

A largely absent father figure is hard to talk back to—except in imagination. The impact of his father's infidelity and neglect of his family were themes Carlos might have softened by describing his father's actions as a "typical Mexican story" in his interview with Steve Heilig. The powerful emotional impact his father's betrayal of his family had on him can be only imagined. Although José and Josefina eventually reunited in Tijuana, José's long absences were still the rule rather than the exception. And due to those repeated and extended absences, Josefina had to practically become a mother who "fathered" Carlos through his tumultuously rebellious teens.

A MOTHER'S MUSICAL INFLUENCE

Josefina had her own way of teaching Carlos a music lesson. José had moved to San Francisco's Mission District, an area with a burgeoning population of Mexican immigrants, with the promise of sending for his family once he was financially established in his new country. In 1961, while the family resided in a number of ramshackle houses in Tijuana, Josefina was the head of the household.

A local band in Tijuana was a far cry from José Santana's mariachi band. The TJs were led by a charismatic lead guitarist, Javier Batiz. They often gave free concerts in town—and Josefina decided that Carlos should hear the group. The TJs played versions of U.S. R&B hits by Chuck Berry and Little Richard, and Carlos was immediately taken by how Batiz played guitar, mingling blues notes with a chunky rhythmic attack. Newly equipped with his father's electric guitar and amp, Carlos asked Batiz for lessons. Opinions differ greatly about what happened next. According to Batiz in a recent interview from his home in Tijuana:

> His mother and a friend brought him [Carlos] over to my house and asked me if I could teach him how to play the guitar like me. I said "yes" and the condition I asked was that I teach him how to play the bass, because I don't have a bass player in my band. So that was it. He was already playing the violin and the acoustic mariachi guitar, but I taught him to play the Electric Blues guitar.[6]

Carlos has downplayed the importance of these music lessons on several occasions, even accusing Batiz of hiding how to play certain guitar chords and disavowing Batiz's influence upon him as a music teacher publicly in a speech given during a ceremony in 2002 when Carlos was given officially the "keys" to the city of Tijuana.[7] Although the facts remain contested, there is no dispute that Batiz was the first teacher Carlos had who played an electric guitar in the style of American rock, and performed electrified blues, and that Josefina brought Batiz and his band to her son's attention. It was Batiz, to some extent, along with his blues idols Muddy Waters and Jimmy Reed (whom Carlos heard on American radio), who provided a major portion of the foundation of his guitar style.

It was during his absence in 1961 that José Santana sent Carlos his first electric guitar and amp. As José Santana remembered the incident years later: in an interview with music journalist Ben Fong-Torres:

> Carlos began to play guitar in the year 1961. When Carlos was nine years of age, he studied in a school of music, after he went to the regular primary school every day. In that music school they wanted Carlos to learn to play the clarinet. He did not like the clarinet, so he began to study violin. But in 1961, when I first came to this country by myself, I bought an electric guitar and amplifier. One year later, when I returned to Mexico, I gave them to Carlos. He became very enthusiastic about the guitar. "Papa, papa, I don't like the violin any more. I like the guitar!" he used to tell me.[8]

The version of this story that Carlos told interviewer Steve Heilig differed in that his father's passing down of his electric guitar was linked to his mother's plea to his father, and that the guitar was "a beat-up old electric guitar," suggesting a somewhat begrudging acknowledgment of his father's gift of the musical instrument that changed Carlos's life.[9] It was with this guitar that Carlos joined a local R&B band, the Strangers, in competition for gigs with the TJs, the band led by his former teacher Batiz. No recordings survive of the Strangers—or of the house band at the El Convoy Club, where Carlos was their featured guitarist. El Convoy was a sleazy and violent strip club where the music, as in strip joints the world over, was secondary to sexual entertainment. Since the blues had long been associated in many Americans' minds with illicit sex, it is not surprising that Carlos found a welcome reception for his blues-saturated guitar among American tourists visiting El Convoy.[10] And among Mexicans visiting El Convoy, they discovered that local blues bands had created the sense that the R&B music of African Americans could be made authentically by Mexicans.

THE SANTANA FAMILY—HAPPY THEY'RE LIVING IN THE U.S.A.?

"I'm so glad I'm livin' in the U.S.A." was a line from a Chuck Berry song on Bay Area radio when the Santana family moved into San

Francisco's Mission District in 1963. Josefina had long wanted to make the move north, believing that her children would have far more educational and career opportunities than their homeland would offer. And the family—with one exception—seemed pleased with their new lives in their new country. Josefina had her husband around the house in a sustained fashion for the first time in years, and their children got to know their father more on a daily basis. But Carlos was anything but happy living in the U.S.A. He wanted to return to Mexico. Carlos's pride was hurt when his English writing skills were judged inferior to those of other fifteen-year-olds and he had to be in junior high school while his peers attended high school. Another factor contributing to the unhappiness Carlos felt in San Francisco was the lack of a regular, paying music gig as the lead guitarist in front of an adult audience nightly. He had transitioned from being musically a "big fish in a small pond" in Tijuana to being "a little fish in a big pond" in San Francisco. As sordid as the atmosphere of El Convoy was, it was a touchstone for pleasing audiences with his blues playing.

A STEP BACKWARD IN ORDER TO MOVE FORWARD

After Carlos nagged his mother repeatedly about how he hated living in San Francisco, she handed him his fare to return to Tijuana. Not unexpectedly, he returned to El Convoy and once more assumed his role as lead guitarist for the house band. He found a place to live through the generosity of a friend of his mother's. As to what kind of music Carlos was playing, it was likely a loud mix of blues and rock full of rhythmic excitement, like T-Bone Walker and Sam "The Man" Taylor. This music wailed with a gritty, sensual tone, suggesting the gradual dramatic build-up of a performer stripping to a big musical beat.

In spite of the musical fulfillment Carlos felt in Tijuana, his family back in San Francisco had enormous misgivings about the fate of a boy his age in such a violent and seductive atmosphere. What happened next becomes, once again and as is often true in family stories fashioned by various family members with different agendas, ambiguous. Carlos told *Rolling Stone* reporter Chris Heath that his mother and big brother Antonio ("Tony") "actually kidnapped me."[11] In the version José told journalist Ben Fong-Torres, José says he went to Tijuana with three other family members and reported, "We did not force him to come. We convinced him by crying."[12]

Regardless of how he ended up reunited with his family in San Francisco, all family members agreed that he was angry to return to the

United States. While his family saw the time Carlos spent living by himself as potentially dangerous, Carlos saw it as a positive step forward in defining his music. Yet his family did correctly believe that San Francisco would offer better educational and economic opportunities for Carlos than he would find in Mexico. And that turned out to be more spectacularly true than anyone in the Santana family could have realized in 1963.

AN ART TEACHER'S FAITH IN CARLOS

Carlos often felt "out of synch" with his fellow students at Mission High School. There was a constant cultural divide and a musical divide between Carlos and his classmates. California teens in the early 1960s strongly favored the pop harmonizing of groups like the Beach Boys, whose lyrics evoked a carefree, harmonious, suburban life punctuated with beach parties and coastal highway driving antics. Although this music categorized as "surf rock" appropriated elements of R&B guitar styles from figures familiar to Carlos, like Chuck Berry, the emphasis on blues notes was rarely underscored. Instead, Dick Dale, the musician credited with inventing the "surf" guitar style, emphasized sharply staccato, "pecking" sounds at high speed, saturated with electrically amplified reverb and distortion. This was a guitar style far removed from that Carlos admired in his blues guitar heroes like B. B. King, where King's notes strongly resembled the human voice laconically moaning or crying. Perhaps influenced by the great jazz vocalist Billie Holiday, King would sometimes play behind the beat of a song, sounding stubbornly unhurried in his execution. On the other hand, Dale and other surf-rock musicians prided themselves on a speedy, "wet," and wavy sound suggestive of surfers riding slightly ahead of cresting waves. King and his fellow bluesmen evoked the dry clarity of a human cry, the wish to triumph over the pain of poverty and racism with an unwaveringly clear voice. King's guitar sound could be interpreted as a guitar equivalent in some ways of the "sorrow songs" of African American slaves that evolved into the spirituals that W.E.B. Du Bois wrote about in *The Souls of Black Folk*. These slave songs were the foundation for what in the twentieth century evolved into African American spirituals, gospel music, and the blues, a musical style placing a premium of the far reaches of vocal ecstasy and/or agony, often sustained to a breaking point.

As Carlos felt detached from his classmates' pop-music tastes, he also felt alienated from their academic interests. As an English-as-a-second-language learner long before the term entered public school curricula,

Carlos was at a distinct disadvantage in subjects where liquid fluency in English reading and writing was assumed. His grades were subpar— except in art and design. Luckily, Carlos had a perceptive art teacher at Mission High School, a Mr. Knudson, who was supportive of both the visual and musical talents of his student.[13] Interestingly, Carlos has long described his music in visual terms, calling his guitar tone "sculpted." He also described his desired guitar sound in these terms: "A note is like a rose," he said. "It can be closed, or halfway open, or all the way in bloom. You have to know when to hit that note the right way—choose how each note is going to be. It's like being a gardener. You want to present the best possible bouquet."[14] So his art teacher seemed to intuit Carlos's artistic vision and helped him find the visual metaphors that allowed him to articulate and shape his musical expression. This ability to experience music as vision is part of a condition psychologists call "synesthesia," a term Carlos had likely never heard at that time, but one historically many gifted musicians have possessed, and a gift he would use throughout his life.

A GRADUAL RECONCILIATION

Carlos completed his public school studies at Mission High School. He made a few friends there and played in a rock band with them. Bass guitarist Gus Rodrigues and drummer Dan Haro, who lived close to Carlos in the Mission District, wanted to form a band to make some money playing at social occasions. Haro's importance in helping Carlos seriously begin his musical career can be attributed to a gift he gave Carlos of a new amplifier. The guitar that Carlos was using in his last years of high school was a Gibson–Les Paul model, the same type of electric guitar played by the English rock guitarists he idolized, Eric Clapton and Peter Green. Unlike acoustic guitarists, electric guitarists cannot fully achieve their individual sound without an amplifier, a potentially costly piece of equipment. Haro's gift was in return for Carlos becoming the group's guitarist, a role Carlos relished. While no recordings survive of the group, which added vocalist Joyce Dunn and concentrated on "soul" hits, it is known that the group finished third in a city-wide "battle of the bands" and introduced Carlos to performing in front of U.S. crowds regularly. "Soul" was a musical style distilled from the rhythm and blues (R&B) of the previous decades, and a mix of blues, gospel, pop, and rock. The superstars of soul were vocalists Otis Redding and Aretha Franklin, artists Carlos listened attentively to on Bay Area radio. Their way of phrasing lyrics, moving between high-pitched wails and partially spoken, sotto sermonizing, caught Carlos's ear and helped inspire his distinctive guitar "cry." Essential, too, to the spell cast by the recordings by these soul vocalists was the electric guitar of Steve Cropper. Cropper's emphasis on single-note runs of great rhythmic force, combined with spare phrases, like pithy verbal asides, had many of the flavors that Carlos loved in blues guitarists like B. B. King. Cropper also knew how to create high drama and suspense within a very brief solo guitar passage and was able to arrange horns on soul records that took the place of guitars. These were all lessons Carlos took seriously.

While he was in school Carlos contributed to the family income by holding down a dishwashing job in a restaurant. Shortly after high school graduation he informed his parents that he needed to get a room for himself and discover his goals. For two years no one in the Santana family knew what had happened to Carlos. Long interested in the hippie counterculture emerging in the Haight-Ashbury section of San Francisco, Carlos was drawn by the emphasis the hippies placed on freedom, sexual, spiritual, and musical, as well as experimentation with hallucinatory drugs like mescaline and LSD. These drugs heightened the sense Carlos had had when he was younger that musical sounds could be seen as constantly mutating visual shapes and colors. For the first time, rock musicians who were connected to the hippie culture performed on stages with a backdrop of projected light shows. These light displays, however loosely synchronized with the live music, were considered faithful to the visionary experience of "tripping" on LSD. Indisputably, this meshing of art and music evoked for Carlos one happy learning experience.

Carlos had a variety of temporary living quarters among the hippies and had his first experiences with consciousness-altering drugs like LSD and mescaline. Carlos found a "guide" or "ambassador" to the drug-saturated countercultural world of the Bay Area in the person of Stan Marcum. A barber by trade, Marcum had a wide knowledge of blues and jazz, even though he had no musical training and played no musical instrument. Marcum helped Carlos interpret the visions Carlos experienced under the influence of psychedelic drugs, and affirmed the sense that Carlos had a special message to give the world through his music. In short, Marcum helped build the solid ego and confidence that Carlos needed in order to enter the music business seriously as a star performer. A certain amount of grandiose self-confidence the Mexican teenager hungered for, Marcum supplied. Marcum also convinced Carlos, at least for a time, that Marcum had the business skills requisite to help Santana's first band be a commercial success. And with Marcum, Carlos could hear what seemed like revolutionary sounds in the jam sessions of drummers at San Francisco's Aquatic Park.

Marcum could help Carlos feel that he belonged to a youthful, musically inspired community built upon unfettered idealism. Hippies did not view experimentation with hallucinatory drugs as self-indulgent but as a brave exploration of cosmic consciousness, a gospel promulgated by ex-Harvard psychology professor Timothy Leary. While Carlos had sound reasons to feel out of place among full-time, politically active students at the University of California at Berkeley and San Francisco State University, largely Caucasian and middle class, he was able to share with them a sense that a new artistic and social consciousness could bring to fruition peace and global harmony.

The Santana family suspected that Carlos was still living within San Francisco city limits—but knew nothing more. Then the silence between Carlos and his family was broken dramatically, as José related:

> Then one day one of my sons heard one of Carlos' songs being played on the radio. "Papa!! It's Carlos!" my son excitedly told me as we listened to the song. The radio announcer kept saying, "Santana! Santana! Santana!"[15]

The family moved into detective mode and discovered that Carlos was still living in San Francisco. Eventually, Carlos called home and invited his family to meet him at the Fillmore West, San Francisco's most prestigious venue for new bands. He was no longer their little boy lost on the streets of Tijuana seeking out a living playing guitar in a sleaze bar. He was now a rock 'n' roll star. The night the Santana family reunited at the Fillmore West was the first contact Carlos had had with his family in two years.

Yet tracing a direct route musically from José's mariachis to the sound Carlos created, first heard by his family on the radio and at the Fillmore West, proves challenging. José was candid in admitting to an interviewer that initially his son's music made no sense to him. What did Carlos do with his Mexican musical roots that made him such a distinctive star internationally? In those years after high school graduation, Carlos discovered a way to condense and synthesize the essence of many life and musical experiences. Carlos untangled the intricate knot of his musical and cultural roots, and then repatterned these roots so he would no longer be a Mexican American rock guitar but a multidimensional world music guitarist. The next chapter in his life story moves deeply into just what roots Carlos had to musically reexamine—and how he forged a new identity for himself in the process.

NOTES

1. Simon Leng, *Soul Sacrifice: The Santana Story* (London: Firefly Publishing, 2000), 11.

2. Marc Shapiro, *Carlos Santana: Back on Top* (New York: St. Martin's Griffin, 2002), 11.

3. Steve Heilig, "The World of Carlos Santana," *The Beat* 19, no. 1 (2000): 43.

4. Experience Music Project/Science Fiction Museum and Hall of Fame, *American Sabor: Latinos in U.S. Popular Music* (Seattle: EMP and SFM, 2007), 10.

5. See Heilig, "The World of Carlos Santana," 3.

6. Fernando Romero, "Batiz Lays Down Indelible Tracks on Tijuana Sound," The Latina Voz, www.latinavoz.com/ArticleArchive.php?ID=34.

7. Ibid. Perhaps tensions between Batiz and Santana have been lessened since 2002 since there is a televised concert on YouTube that shows Batiz performing a cover of Santana's "I Love You Much Too Much" (!) in which Batiz hands his guitar over to Carlos in order to complete the last chorus of the song. See http://vids.myspace.com/index.cfm?fuseaction=vids.individual&VideoID=16934684.

8. Ben Fong-Torres, *Not Fade Away: A Backstage Pass to 20 Years of Rock and Roll* (San Francisco: Miller Freeman, 1999), 104.

9. Heilig, "World of Carlos Santana," 44.

10. See Paul Oliver, *Screening the Blues* (New York: Da Capo Books, 1989), for an extended analysis of sexual themes in the blues Carlos was most familiar with.

11. Chris Heath, "The Epic Life of Carlos Santana," *Rolling Stone*, March 16, 2000, 44.

12. Fong-Torres, *Not Fade Away*, 104.

13. Shapiro, *Carlos Santana*, 48.

14. Carlos Santana biography, SF Mission website, http://www.sfmission.com/santana/earlyears.htm.

15. Fong-Torres. *Not Fade Away*, 105.

Chapter 2

MEXICAN BLUES ARRIVE AT WOODSTOCK

HOW THE SANTANA SOUND EMERGED

"My father taught me how to get inside the note," noted Carlos in a recent interview. "When you get inside the note, you put your fingerprints on it."[1] This is the key to why in a career spanning four decades, Santana remains a musical giant for generations of fans. In a popular music scene where so many guitarists fall into rigidly formulaic styles and sound the same, the distinctive and ever-evolving cry of Santana's guitar rings out for listeners sensing that this is music nourishing the soul.

How did Santana get inside a musical note and put his distinctive fingerprints on it? The answer begins to come into focus as music fans learn, as Carlos Santana did, about the African roots of the blues. The blues might seem an odd part of the Carlos Santana story, a story so connected to his Mexican heritage and his fame as the first Latin rock international superstar. But the first successful band that Carlos Santana led, in San Francisco in the 1960s, was called "The Santana Blues Band." And much as Carlos has acknowledged how his father drilled him musically in practicing Western classical music, he has also wryly noted his indebtedness to a different "three Bs": "You'd be surprised how much time I spend with the Paul Butterfield band's *East-West* too. That album was a major groundbreaker. The three B's—Butterfield, Bloomfield, and Bishop were scary, man! They opened up the entire spectrum."[2] The Paul Butterfield Blues Band was also responsible for the first time Carlos performed on stage at the Fillmore West, cementing those deep roots of the blues for Carlos.

To better understand how Carlos developed his unique reworking of the blues guitar tradition, it is illuminating to go to the bedrock, the deep roots of the Mexican musical heritage that Carlos originally learned from his father. While no respected music historian has ever claimed that the blues originated in Mexico, there is an intriguing possibility that some flavor of that musical style—particularly the musical "cry"—traveled centuries ago from Africa through Spain and then to the New World.

Four fascinating albums by leading musical authorities explore the connection between the blues and Africa. They include *Roots of the Blues: Some Correspondences between the Music of the Slave Areas of West Africa and the Music of the United States and the Caribbean* compiled by Samuel Charters, *Black Music of Two Worlds* collected by John Storm Roberts, and *Yonder Comes the Blues* culled by Paul Oliver. But in order to best appreciate swiftly the tie between the blues' "cry" and traditional African music the album to start with is *Roots of the Blues*, collected by the famous world music scholar Alan Lomax. The album opens with the sound of Henry Ratcliff, an African American prisoner forced to pick crops under a blazing Mississippi sun. His song, which Lomax recorded in the open air, was made up spontaneously and unaccompanied by musical instruments. Music scholars call it a "field holler" or "work holler" and it does sound exactly like a man who is being worked to exhaustion rallying his spirits in order to survive. It is easy to imagine slaves in Mississippi a century before Lomax recorded Ratcliff making up like songs that were hollers and shouts encouraging themselves to "keep on keepin' on."

In producing this album, Lomax decided to do a little experiment. He edited the Ratcliff recording so that only a snippet is heard at first. Then Lomax followed it immediately with an excerpt from a Senegalese rice harvester who also made up a work song on the spot reflecting his feelings about having to work so hard in such intense heat. The singer from Africa sings in a language we can't understand, but his tune and tone are so close to that of the American prisoner that it sounds like the two participated in a musical conversation. They both sounded like they had the blues—as we would too if we had to work under the conditions they did. Their musical cry binds them. And it is easy to conjecture that when slaves were cruelly transported by ship over centuries between Africa and the Western hemisphere that the slaves remembered the melodies and rhythms of their African heritage when they arrived in the New World. These African musical roots transplanted to Mexico and the United States are exactly what Carlos shows a sharp awareness of when he says in an interview: "And, you know, again, the roots of all our music comes from Africa."[3]

How did these African roots of the blues blossom for Carlos? The transformation began with the rock 'n' roll that Carlos heard as a boy. That was his first awakening to his true musical identity. He wanted to play guitar in a rock 'n' roll band, a fact that his father recognized and so gave Carlos his first guitar. As a passionate listener to U.S. radio stations in the late 1950s and early 1960s, he quickly realized that many rock guitarists were playing electric guitar in a style inherited from blues musicians from Mississippi, Memphis, Texas, and Chicago. Particularly catching his ear were Bobby Parker, B. B. King, Freddie King, and Lightnin' Hopkins. It is helpful to remember that as Carlos entered his teen years many of the powerful California radio stations that could be received in Mexico were broadcasting what was then identified as "Negro" music, an umbrella term encompassing not just blues and early rock 'n' roll, but gospel and jazz as well.

Reflecting the racial and cultural atmosphere of that time, white radio deejay Hunter Hancock on KGFJ in Los Angeles made the multigenre nature of southern California "Negro music" radio explicit, playing music from jazz diva Dinah Washington to rocker Chuck Berry to an overwhelmingly African American community of listeners.[4] Seven years later KGFJ would become one of the first radio stations in the country to employ disc jockeys of both races to play rock 'n' roll. Santana's band would be the first multiracial rock band to make the big time.

In addition to guitarists imitating a human cry with their instruments, blues musicians also began to imitate a range of human "voices": fast chatter, whispers, slurs, moans, and interjections of surprise and passion. Before electric guitars were invented, acoustic guitarists developed these effects through a variety of mechanical means. The "bottleneck" technique Carlos has used throughout his career referred originally to an actual beer-bottle neck, broken off from the bottle and sanded, and used as a device to press and slide down all guitar strings simultaneously. This gives an acoustic guitar a zingy, propulsively dynamic sound. Another acoustic guitar technique that brings about unusual vocal tones involves "choking" the strings, pushing them to one side of the fret board intensely while pressing them down on the guitar's fret board. And yet another acoustic guitar technique involves playing close to or below the guitar's bridge.

The electric guitar introduced a vast array of vocal tones unavailable to acoustic guitarists through various amplifiers, pick-ups, and sundry accessories (e.g., wah-wah pedals, whammy bars, and so on). Electric guitar sounds could also be thunderously loud, meaning that the notes could fill huge halls and could be sustained far longer than was possible with an acoustic guitar. Any loud and sustained electric guitar sound, and this becomes increasingly true the higher the note pitch, creates an intensely overwhelming emotional jolt, the sonic equivalent of a rush of adrenalin. That was one reason why electric guitar playing spawned the revolutionary style of rock.

The rock 'n' roll that thrilled Carlos as a teenager was an outgrowth of the blues that began in the South, the Mississippi delta, Texas, and Memphis and gradually spread to northern cities, particularly Kansas City and Chicago. That migration north literally and symbolically *electrified* the blues. In the words of one of Carlos's musical heroes from the Mississippi delta, the bluesman Muddy Waters, "The blues had a baby and they called it rock and roll." And while music fans will never know exactly all of the rock 'n' roll young Carlos heard, we do know from his own accounts that he was listening to a variety of performers who began careers playing traditional blues and transformed themselves into "rhythm and blues" performers acceptable for mass radio consumption. The line dividing "rhythm and blues" and rock 'n' roll from the 1950s on was often blurred, so it is fair to think of four of the greatest musicians impacting Carlos, Chuck Berry, Bo Diddley, Bobby Parker, and B. B. King, as early rock musicians by the 1960s as much as great bluesmen with superb guitar artistry. They were "rocking" the formerly steady blues beat, making the blues more rhythmically driving, making it music to energetically dance to.

A frenetic rock beat dominated the airwaves during Carlos's adolescence, perhaps reflecting the giddy optimism of that period of economic growth in the United States. But for Carlos in Mexico, poverty and mariachi music constituted everyday reality. So the rhythmic jolt of rock 'n' roll catapulted his dreams of becoming a great guitarist. And the blues elements found in the guitar solos of B. B. King and Chuck Berry gave voice to his frustrations about living in an environment where the ground seemed always too near for a young musician with ambitious dreams reaching toward the sky. The sounds of their wailing, blues-saturated electric guitars gave Carlos permission to rebel against his family past.

A BONGO FROM LIVERPOOL ECHOING IN SAN FRANCISCO

In addition to this blues-flavored rock 'n' roll, a particular song of quite a different style caught his teenage enthusiasm. Later he eloquently

talked about it in a documentary film about the history of his music entitled *Viva Santana*. Amazingly, the song that deeply inspired Carlos
was the 1964 hit by the Beatles, "And I Love Her," a somewhat Latin-
sounding ballad written by Paul McCartney and John Lennon. But what
caught young Carlos's ear was drummer Ringo Starr playing bongo drums
instead of his usual drum kit in the recording studio. Interestingly, this
fact did not immediately spark in Carlos the desire to play with bongo
drummers. That moment would not blossom into reality until he developed his unique musical signature in the San Francisco area in the late
1960s. But it was a significant moment of opening his awareness that
rock 'n' roll did not always have to be performed with one drummer
playing a single steady rhythm on a conventional drum kit.

   Ringo Starr's use of the bongo carried a symbolic as well as musical
meaning. Both in the United Kingdom and the United States, young
people in the late 1950s and early 1960s who were actively rebelling
against the political and social values of earlier generations performed
their original poetry accompanied by bongo drums. Bongo drum
rhythms were first associated with beatniks, then with hippies (whom
Carlos would come to know intimately during his early years in the
Bay Area). Since both the beatnik and hippie movements were largely
composed of white, middle-class WASP (White Anglo-Saxon Protes-
tant) youth, they were unaware of the importance of the instrument in
the context of Latin jazz. This genre was most appreciated by Americans of Latin descent who mainly lived in the northeastern United
States where a form of popular dance music known as "salsa," based on
Afro-Cuban sacred dance rhythms, began to emerge as Carlos moved
through his teenage musical apprenticeship. Yet as Latin music historian Raul Fernandez noted, "during the 1950s, several important percussionists in the Afro-Cuban tradition, notably Armando Peraza,
Mongo Santamaria, and Willie Bobo, moved to the Bay area."[5]
Although Carlos was unaware of this "holy trinity" of Afro-Cuban
drummers in California, he would have the opportunity to play alongside them once his career was in high gear. As a teenager, he was
unaware that a wave of jazz with Latin tinges had been performed and
recorded in San Francisco by Cal Tjader, Vince Guaraldi, Mango Santamaria, and Willie Bobo long before his U.S. arrival. Bobo, born William Correa in 1934 in Spanish Harlem in New York to Puerto Rican
parents, was the composer of the Santana band's first hit, "Evil Ways,"
having recorded it with a studio band using the name "Willie Bobo" to
moderate notice in 1967. Bobo did not cross paths with Carlos until he
joined the Santana band for a brief stint during the 1970s.

Not all bongo players were Latin jazz professionals or beatniks on their way to becoming hippies. Some were students at the politically turbulent University of California–Berkeley campus where a variety of students jammed on drums as an act of political protest on a campus where they felt they had little direct voice in the policies of their school. Some of these students would come to the first Santana shows at the Fillmore in San Francisco. And running that venue was a figure that would loom large through three decades of Carlos's musical career: Bill Graham.

BILL GRAHAM SETS THE STAGE

Graham, born Wolodia Granjonca to Russian Jewish parents, was, like the superstar he would manage, no stranger to family trauma in early childhood. Graham's father died in a freakish accident within a week of his son's birth, and Graham's mother was killed in a Nazi concentration camp. Graham's reaction to the loss of his mother was to flee on foot across war-ravaged Europe to a ship that carried him from Lisbon, Portugal, to the United States. Raised by foster parents in New York City, Graham hustled his way through a number of jobs before making his way as a music business entrepreneur in San Francisco. It was at Graham's venue, the Fillmore, that an ambitious teenage guitarist from Mexico asked through a friend, Stan Marcum, if he could jam with the musicians on stage. Little could Graham have known that the boy about to perform on his club's stage that night would evolve into a star with a "rags to riches" story uncannily mirroring Graham's.

It was a bold move on Carlos's part to push his way onto the Fillmore's concert stage. His sole previous appearance on a San Francisco stage had been at a teenage "battle of the bands" where Carlos with drummer Dan Haro, bassist Gus Rodrigues, and vocalist Joyce Dunn were quickly deemed substandard compared to their garage-band peers by the evening's judges. Being drunk while auditioning certainly didn't help their competitive edge and musical execution. It was quite a different scene at the Fillmore. On stage that night was an outstanding assortment of nationally recognized professional musicians with deep roots in the blues, the Paul Butterfield Blues Band from Chicago. Unfortunately, Butterfield, the band's leader and harmonica player, showed up on stage in a drugged state that made it clear to his band members that he would be incapable of playing that night. When Carlos asked Graham if he could jam with the established musicians onstage,

Graham pointed to guitarist and keyboardist Michael Bloomfield and said, "It's not my decision. Ask Bloomfield. If he says you can play, you can."

Carlos was not a stranger to Graham at this defining moment in 1965. For months, Carlos and his high school friends had been pestering Graham to let them in to hear their musical heroes, like Eric Clapton, free of charge since the Santana family was living hand-to-mouth in those days. But what of Carlos as a serious musician? Whatever thought Graham had at that moment by transferring the decision about Carlos performing to Bloomfield, it proved to be a revelation for Graham and many in the audience that night. "The skinny Mexican kid" no one had heard on stage in the United States before became an overnight rock-blues guitar sensation. Graham asked Carlos if he had a band and if he would be interested in performing at the Fillmore. Carlos stretched the truth and informed Graham that, yes, he did have a band, and furiously set about organizing one, which became "The Santana Blues Band."

Rock-blues in the mid-sixties often showcased long jams, loose improvisations where guitars might duel for a half hour in the middle of a song. There was little to no room for improvisation in his father's mariachi band, but it was a linchpin of Santana's musical obsession. That might explain his father's note of bewilderment when his son's first album, *Santana*, was released. He remarked, "I listened to my son's record—but I have to be frank. I can't tell where the songs begin or end."[6]

Improvisational rock was an essential first step toward Carlos becoming a multidimensional musician. In improvisation, a musician is composing and performing simultaneously, and doing so while carefully listening to his or her fellow band members. It requires, paradoxically, enormously sophisticated musical knowledge and skill—and the ability to occasionally step free of many or most of the conventional rules of music. It has been most common in jazz over the past century. Only during the 1960s, as Carlos came of age, did improvisation become a part of rock 'n' roll, particularly among bands in the Bay Area. The recording companies' willingness to include tunes outside the mold of the usual three-minute hit song intended for AM radio listeners or young music fans with short attention spans was responsible for the increasing emphasis on rock improvisation. FM radio, responding to a new generation of sophisticated rock fans, favored programming long album selections. So the airwaves became filled with lengthy expositions of rock music.

At the Fillmore Carlos got to hear fellow San Francisco musicians of his generation, the Grateful Dead, Jefferson Airplane, Quicksilver Messenger Service, and Sly and the Family Stone. And although the

Butterfield Blues Band generally eschewed long improvisational blues jams, their 1966 album *East-West* had a lasting impact on Carlos and other San Francisco rockers (in fact, in 2005 Carlos told an interviewer *East-West* was an album he was still listening carefully to). The title tune was a 13-minute improvisation showcasing two electric guitarists, Michael Bloomfield and Elvin Bishop, playing a mélange of blues, rock, and Indian sitar music, apparently learned through listening to recordings of the burgeoning Indian sitar player Ravi Shankar. In addition to inspiring Carlos, it strongly impacted other Bay Area rock bands. The Grateful Dead recorded "Dark Star," a blues-jazz-rock extended jam with touches of Eastern musical modes interpenetrating blues riffs. And key members of the Jefferson Airplane, guitarist Jorma Kaukonen and bassist Jack Casady, enjoyed long bluesy solos that led to them forming their own blues-jam band, Hot Tuna, by 1969, yet another fruitful off-shoot of the Butterfield Band's inspiration.

GUITARISTS FROM ENGLAND SHOW CARLOS A PATH

Musical visitors from England also played in San Francisco. One was a young rock guitarist from Seattle who had to relocate himself in England to order to gain attention in his native land, and whose rock and blues guitar playing would leave an indelible mark on Carlos's career. That was Jimi Hendrix, the most daring electric guitar improvisator ever heard when his first album debuted in 1967. Carlos began making homemade tapes of Hendrix's performances and maintains his collection for inspiration today. Many guitarists and music critics believe Hendrix has never been surpassed in improvisational genius on electric guitar. Hendrix realized that a symphonic range of musical colors and textures could be drawn from an electric guitar through artful use of electronic distortion, achingly long sustained notes, and shatteringly bright, lyrically piercing treble notes, presented in cascading showers like a fireworks display. Through careful study of blues masters B. B. King and Howlin' Wolf, Hendrix was able to make his guitar imitate their vocal rasps and yells.

The other guitarist who had a formidable impact on the shaping of Carlos's playing was a young English guitarist, Peter Green (born Greenbaum). Green, like another one of Carlos's guitar models, Eric Clapton, had honed his blues guitar skills within John Mayall and the Bluesbreakers, a highly popular English blues band. Green left Mayall to start his own band, Fleetwood Mac, and released a song in 1966, "Black Magic Woman," that would later provide Carlos the second huge hit of his career. Interestingly, Green, during his Fillmore shows, would often showcase another original number with a guitar solo that sounded like a cross between B. B. King and the mature Carlos Santana, entitled "Supernatural." It is likely that the title of Carlos's internationally bestselling, Grammy-winning album reflected a tip of the hat to Green. Although his career was seriously aborted during the 1970s due to drug and mental health problems, Green still plays today, though not with his original creative genius, and shared the stage with Carlos when both were inducted into the Rock and Roll Hall of Fame in 1998.

Green's guitar style was quite different from that of Hendrix. While Hendrix was wildly splashy and extroverted in adding bravura and downright vulgar flourishes to simple blues at a fevered pitch, and favored quoting pop melodies in a fractured way, Green was carefully restrained, introverted, and economically succinct, letting a small number of notes serve as suggestive hints of tasteful flourishes to come. The raging singing tone at the center of Hendrix's playing was more a menacing hum at the center of Green's, exemplified by his solos with the John Mayall and the Bluesbreakers album, A Hard Road. Both Hendrix and Green were able to improvise with enormous taste and intelligence within the framework of blues-rock.

HOW FREE MUSICALLY COULD CARLOS BECOME?

Essential to playing highly improvisatory music is a strong need for freedom from rigidly fixed musical forms. The term "jam session," used to describe musical events marked by long stretched of improvised music, originated in the 1930s as jazz players enjoyed an enhanced sense of freedom from former musical conventions. The spawning of improvisational rock in the Bay Area was reflective of its long history in exploring new forms of everyday living, a consequence of much "thinking outside the box." During his teen years in the Mission District, Carlos found friends whose experimental lifestyles included the recreational use of hallucinatory drugs and sexual experiences outside of societal conventions. Bay Area band members of the Grateful Dead and Jefferson Airplane used hallucinatory drugs on the assumption that drugs like LSD offered a doorway into a "free-form" musical consciousness and provided an easy rationale for playing music without any apparent formal constraints.

It was not until Carlos was seriously introduced to major jazz recordings by John Coltrane and Miles Davis by his accomplished drummer

Michael Shrieve that he realized how musical improvisation was a highly disciplined act and that his music would never be "free" of "form." He learned through Miles Davis that musical form could be elastic and more like a cloud in motion than a box with rigid walls. But initially, the promise of LSD offering a utopian vision of free-form guitar improvisation, bringing music "in tune" with the cosmos, was as emotionally thrilling for Carlos as it was for many other rock guitarists his age. T-shirts sold briskly in San Francisco during the sixties boldly proclaiming the glories of "sex, drugs, and rock 'n' roll." For Carlos, that was a kind of holy trinity temporarily substituting for the Trinity of his parents' Mexican Catholicism.

As was common to many artistically creative teenagers at that time, Carlos found a guide to alternative music and lifestyle corners in the Bay Area through his friendship with Stan Marcum. Marcum was not a musician—but a friend to many. In spite of his lack of either music or business experience, he became the manager of the first Santana band. Marcum brought three musicians into the first incarnation of the Santana band. Bassist David Brown made a solid contribution to the band's first three commercially successful albums. Drummers Bob "Doc" Livingston and conga player Marcus Malone were mundane and unreliable compared to the percussionists who followed in their wake, and never were heard on any of Santana's hit albums. But by bringing in percussionists who could play Afro-Latin rhythm, Marcum helped shape the lifetime direction of Carlos's music, fusing explicitly the African and blues themes.

This penchant for drug-induced free-form guitar jams never sat well with Graham, the commercially savvy promoter. Perhaps he grew tired of hearing so many unfocused jam sessions at the Fillmore. Also, the Latin music that Graham loved from recordings, mambos and salsa by Tito Puente and Celia Cruz, rarely showcased very lengthy jam sessions. Graham repeatedly advised Santana to reign in improvisational energies and produce radio-friendly songs. It was Graham, a long-time Latin music fan, who introduced Willie Bobo's recording of "Evil Ways" to Santana, insisting that the Santana band record it because of the song's potential for a smash hit. Graham was absolutely correct in that assessment. "Evil Ways" was a mild "crossover" hit for its composer, the percussionist Bobo, "crossover" referring in this case to a commercially viable blend of Latin rhythms and pop vocals and lyrics. The words are little more than a man's heavy-handed accusation imploring his woman to change "her evil ways" (e.g., gossiping and cheating on him).

It was also a song that helped Carlos contend with reconciling contentious factions within his band. The original Santana band, which had a smash-hit album, featured drummer Michael Shrieve and keyboardist Gregg Rolie, both of whom loved jazz; David Brown, a bassist deeply connected with blues; and percussionists Michael Carabello and José "Chepito" Areas, obsessed with Latin dance music. The band members could only find cohesion through their shared love of improvisation—yet they knew that Graham was correct that they would not find their music profitable until they could simplify it into concise songs. In order to do so, the electric guitar would need to soar over the rhythm section with an energetic flamboyance, rocking the band's stylistic indebtedness to the blues and Latin music.

Columbia Records, the record label Santana recorded with until 1989, released an interesting (and the only legally authorized) recording of the earliest incarnation of the Santana band that played at the Fillmore in 1968. The liner notes by Alan di Perna claim, "It's clear that the classic Santana sound had coalesced by the time these recordings were made."[7] This is a highly debatable claim. The band consisted of only one percussionist, Marcus Malone, and one drummer, Bob "Doc" Livingston. Neither percussionist had impressive agility with the tricky polyrhythms of Latin music. Bassist David Brown and keyboardist and vocalist Gregg Rolie, present in 1968, did transition into the first internationally acclaimed Santana band. If anything in this recording supports the idea that Carlos and band circa 1968 had solidified their sound, it can be found in the interplay between Carlos and keyboardist Rolie. As Rolie commented in a 1997 interview, "Carlos had never played with a guitarist who could do his own stuff—who could jam. Some of the lines we used were supposed to be horn lines. But we only had an organ and a guitar. So we would be simulating it in our heads."[8] Strangely, when Carlos wanted to add horns to the band during the recording of *Santana III*, many band numbers objected on the grounds that the original Santana band sound was not driven by horns. Rolie and Santana's musical friendship kept the band performing at its peak for years. And when Rolie left to join the band Journey in the 1970s, his subsequent replacements on keyboards, Tom Coster and Chester Thompson, had equally creative musical contributions that unified those later editions of the Santana band.

A justification for Columbia Records releasing a tape so long in their vaults was giving Santana fans the opportunity to hear how eminently danceable the band's repertoire was from the start. Even with the technical shortcomings of the Malone-Livingston percussion section, the

band projected an inviting Latin-flavored rock sound. Carlos notes of
his music of that time in the *Live at the Fillmore 68* CD booklet, "When
we played, the women would dance differently. All of a sudden, they
would start moving their hips in a sensuous way, moving their bodies
like they were belly dancing." This connection between the Santana
band sound and Latin dancing was a fulfillment of a dance and music
trend of the 1950s.

AN AFRICAN DRUMMER CALLS OUT TO CARLOS

Babatunje Olatunji, a Nigerian drummer of great talent and show-
manship, had moved to the United States in the 1950s, and Columbia
Records released a highly influential recording of his African drumming, *Drums of Passion*, in 1959. While the widespread availability of
African recordings, particularly of drumming, is taken for granted in
the twenty-first century, Olatunji's album caused a stir on its release
since it was the first widely available commercial recording of African
drumming. Beatniks and, later, hippies would identify the sounds of
that album with free love and drug trips. Reflecting a more serious
slant, the album was immediately popularized through African dance
and dance therapy classes in the Bay Area. So when the Santana band
performed "Jingo," their rocking rearrangement of Olatunji's "Gin-
Go-Lo-Ba," at the Fillmore in 1968, the rhythmic, chant-and-trance-
inducing tune had already been familiar to numerous dance students
and social dancers for nearly a decade.

The fact that Carlos could instantly draw a connection between the
African and Latin rhythms infusing his music, and cast a sensually seductive spell upon his female fans, connected him more deeply to his
father than perhaps he realized at the time. His father had courted his
mother by serenading her with a love ballad on the street outside her
window. On a more disturbing note, José's extramarital romances outside his home town were fueled by his musical career often taking him
on tour. Carlos made the family lore about musicianship and romanc-
ing explicit in a healthy way by having his father record the same song
he courted his mother with, "Vereda Tropical," for the most autobiographical album Carlos ever made, *Havana Moon* (1983).

Romance aside, and Carlos often chastised his fellow band members
for spending too much time partying with their girlfriends and not
enough time perfecting their musicianship, Carlos was learning to
appreciate hours of disciplined practice. He wanted to play in a band
where musical devotion on the part of its members was pitched as

intensely as his, an authentic community of dedicated musicians. For that reason, in 1969 he dismissed Livingston, who suffered a variety of drug-related lapses on stage, and Malone, who had a number of serious psychological problems. Their removal was triggered by a difficult time attempting to make an album for the Atlantic label under the guidance of producer David Rubinson. Rubinson was disgusted by the band's lack of professionalism and dismayed by the lackluster recordings the band created. That led Carlos to realize that a rhythm section equal to his own musical commitment was an urgent need.

It was a smart move. Percussionist Michael Carabello, who had previous experience playing with Santana, was brought back into the fold to replace Malone. And Carabello knew a Nicaraguan percussionist, José "Chepito" (Spanish for "chipmunk, referring to José's small stature) Areas, who added decades of experience working in a wide range of Latin music groups. Even more spectacular was the replacement of Livingston with Michael Shrieve. Through his teen years Shrieve had carefully listened to recordings by jazz titans Miles Davis and John Coltrane. He was able to integrate the polyrhythmic styles of the key drummers who played with Davis (Tony Williams) and Coltrane (Elvin Jones). Jazz bandleaders from the 1920s on liked to call their drummers "the engine room." Drums in rock, as well as jazz, have been the rhythmic "fuel" in a band's engine. And with Carabello, Areas, and Shrieve driving the Santana band's engine room, the band was ready to go into musical overdrive.

WHAT'S IN A NAME?

One question that was plaguing this newly recharged version of the Santana band was the band's name. In and of itself, this first appeared as a trivial issue. The rules of the San Francisco Musicians Union, which Carlos and his fellow musicians were members of, required every band to have a designated leader and name. "Santana" was chosen as a quick remedy to satisfy the union's requirement. But this proved to be a fateful decision for the band in a number of positive and negative ways. Positively, the name, which means "saint-like" in Spanish, proclaimed the rock band as proudly Latino, a first in the history of rock 'n' roll. Carlos was not the first Latin superstar in rock. That distinction belonged to Ritchie Valens, whose all-too-brief career ended at age 17 in a tragic plane crash, leaving behind the legacy of one song, "La Bamba." But Carlos foregrounded Latin rock by being the first to have a Latino band name on marquees around the world. By using his family name for the band's name, Carlos once again kept a thread between himself and his family, however tenuous the relationship was in reality Negatively, the name raised questions as to whether Carlos was the unquestioned leader of the group—or one of six equal co-creators. This problem would dog the group through their first three albums, the eponymous *Santana*, *Abraxas*, and *Santana III*. So acrimonious were the arguments among Carlos and his musicians when these hit albums were created between 1969 and 1971 that many members of this version of the Santana band refused to talk or musically collaborate with Carlos for decades. When this version of the Santana band regrouped to re-cord in the 1990s, Carlos declined the opportunity to join them again. Their own group, Abraxas Pool, was named for the *Abraxas* album, which remains Carlos's sentimental favorite of the 45 group and solo albums he recorded. But Abraxas Pool, essentially the first Santana band without the guitarist that gave them their original band moniker, released an album that attracted little notice. Without Carlos's pres-ence and name attached to the project, commercial success was not achieved.

Before the Santana band went into Columbia's recording studio to record their first smash album, a number of the band members thought they would be better off musically without Carlos. In spite of the saintly family name, Carlos could be very vociferously argumentative about what the band's sound needed to be. These arguments were likely fueled by drugs as well as by the financial and management pressures exerted upon them. Bill Graham was pressuring Carlos to convince his colleagues to reduce their free-form jams and go for a commercial hit. Bassist David Brown was strongly into the soul music of James Brown and wanted Santana to reach deeply into that Ray Charles–James Brown kind of crowd-pleasing soul and blues sound. Michael Shrieve was pushing for more jazz rhythms.

Graham helped save the day in one small and one spectacularly big way. An abrasive contrarian, Graham loudly and repeatedly insisted the band make a radio hit through adopting a relatively simple Latin tune, "Evil Ways," by Willie Bobo. Knowing the original 1961 record-ing well, Graham realized the potential of highlighting Carlos's guitar lines and Rolie's organ lines as substitutes for the trumpets and a tenor sax (that offers the tune's only solo) in Bobo's original. The lyrics were throwaway, but lyrical profundity was not the point. Graham further realized the tune could easily transfigured into an original rock hit by having short, punchy guitar lines counterpointed by authentic Latin dance patterns, in tight synch with a predictably steady, 4/4 rock beat.

BY THE TIME THEY GOT TO WOODSTOCK

The most spectacular gift Graham gave the band was a prominent spot at the Woodstock Music and Art Fair in 1969. Through shrewd wheeling and dealing with the festival's organizers, Graham managed to get the band on the history-making performer roster in spite of the fact that the group had no album available at the time for sale and were unknown outside of the Bay Area. Although Graham had no fore-knowledge, any more than the event's organizers, that the festival would bring over a half million music fans from around the world, Graham was aware that over 30 bands with global reputations were on the bill. And he suspected it would be the ultimate showcase and com-ing-out party for Santana.

And it was. Santana played on the festival's second day, Saturday, August 16, 1969, a seven-song set that included six tunes that would appear on their first album: "Waiting," "You Just Don't Care," "Savor," "Jingo," "Persuasion," and "Soul Sacrifice." Only "Fried Neckbones," a tune recorded earlier by Willie Bobo, was not included on their debut recording. The film of the festival shows a rather disinterested recep-tion to the MC's announcement of Santana coming on stage because so few of the half-million music fans had ever heard of them. The crowd quickly warmed to the group, particularly the women, whose dancing likely brought back to Carlos memories of the women dancing during his first Bay Area concerts. The Santana instrumental showcase, "Soul Sacrifice," which is featured in the film *Woodstock*, was clearly the highpoint of the band's shining debut. As captured on film, a furi-ously passionate camaraderie ripples through the band's electrifying performance. Drummer Michael Shrieve's drumming is especially inspired, and the interplay between Carlos and organist Gregg Rolie is also remarkable. The tune is a rhythmic tour de force with many layers of Latin and rock rhythm careening off one another as Carlos's guitar soars above the fray. The piece speedily accelerates like a locomotive gaining momentum with every passing minute—then stops suddenly, unexpectedly—then picks up momentum again. It didn't possess a memorable melody line—but succeeded through sheer torque, through blazing polyrhythms tied together by a guitarist Latinizing the blues cry.

The *Woodstock* film also captures Carlos's facial expressions while he solos. He looks like a young man in quick locomotion between the ecstasies and agonies of spiritual transcendence or romantic lust. Part of that look of spiritual transcendence was actually a consequence of

Carlos having ingested the hallucinatory drug mescaline soon before the band was unexpectedly called on stage. Some of those facial grimaces Carlos displays were a consequence of imagining that his guitar had morphed into a snake he was trying to control. Nevertheless, he possessed the photogenic charms of a rock world celebrity, a fact that wouldn't escape Graham's attention, or that of the women attracted by his onstage charisma. How that charismatic look was both a blessing and curse will be revealed as Santana's story unfolds over the years. One thing was obvious: in pop music looking good was as vital as good playing—and Carlos covered both bases.

The Woodstock performance was a triumph for Carlos and his colleagues—but only one of many to follow. The deep significance of their Woodstock experience gradually became apparent when they went into the studio to record their first album for Columbia. That recording proved that Carlos and his band were ready for the long odyssey of becoming rock 'n' roll stars of originality and perennial appeal across national, musical, and generational boundaries.

NOTES

1. Interview with Carlos Santana on *Supernatural Live* DVD (Aviva 07822-15750-9, 2000).

2. Darrin Fox, "Carlos Santana Spreads the Gospel of Tone," *Guitar Player*, May 2005. Retrieved from www.guitarplayer.com/article/carlos-santana-spreads/May-05/8870.

3. Heilig, "World of Carlos Santana," 46.

4. The oldies collection CD *Cruisin' 1959* (Increase Records, 1993) includes a recording of Hunter Hancock's introduction, where he specifies that he plays "Negro" music.

5. Raul Fernandez, *Latin Jazz: The Perfect Combination* (San Francisco: Chronicle Books, 2002), 77.

6. Ben Fong-Torres, *Not Fade Away: A Backstage Pass to 20 Years of Rock and Roll* (San Francisco: Miller Freeman, 1999), 105.

7. Alan di Perna, liner notes for *Santana: Live at the Fillmore '68* (Columbia Legacy C2K 64860, 1997).

8. Ibid.

Chapter 3

COSTS OF FAME AND FORTUNE

THE FIRST THREE HIT ALBUMS: PEAKS AND VALES FOR SANTANA

The first three albums by Santana were products of a stable core of musicians. Carlos did all of the lead guitar work while Gregg Rolie handled keyboards and vocals. David Brown played bass while the thundering percussion section comprised Michael Shrieve on trap drums, Michael Carabello on conga drum, and Chepito Areas on conga and timbales. To what extent the band's auspicious hit-making start represented a synthesis of all six players is a point still hot debated among the musicians, their fans, and critics.

In an interview Carlos clearly delimited the reason for the band's early success: "the nucleus was still Gregg Rolie and I."[1] This perspective was understandable considering the musical influences Rolie brought to Carlos. Further in the same interview, Carlos credited Rolie with tuning him into recordings by Jimmy Smith, Paul McCartney, and Mick Jagger. In essence, Carlos acknowledged that Rolie enhanced his awareness of the beauty of catchy melodies (McCartney), the importance of blues-rock (Jagger), and the need for jazz improvisation between guitar and organ, marked with R&B, soul, and funk tonal colors (Smith).

Curiously, the first Santana album seemed the most remote from these influences. It was heavily caught up with Carlos's rock electric-guitar solos against the backdrop of layers of African and Afro-Caribbean percussion. The hit single from the album, "Evil Ways," did allow for Carlos and Rolie to exchange tasty musical licks, but the longer tunes that attracted FM radio DJ and listener attention were guitar and Latin percussion jams. "Jingo," a cover of a furiously drummed and chanted composition by the Nigerian drummer Olatunji, fit that description. So did the tune that galvanized their half-million listeners at the Woodstock Musical Festival in 1969, "Soul Sacrifice," a hit, given the crowd's response before the first Santana album was released.

Carlos's insistence that the earliest version of the band was a guitar and keyboard–driven unit can be understood in terms of Carlos only gradually perceiving the uniqueness of the band's sound in terms of the balanced counterpoint between his bluesy lead guitar work and African and Caribbean rhythms. Carlos called his first band "The Santana Blues Band," a name that didn't suggest Afro-Caribbean musical styles at all. As Carlos related to interviewer Steve Heilig, he wasn't aware of the East Coast salsa scene that heavily featured Afro-Cuban sounds at the time he started his band.[2]

The original Santana band line-up of the initial three albums only cohered through the band members' willingness to learn from one another. As Rolie was intently learning licks from listening to the Beatles, the Rolling Stones, and Jimmy Smith, Carlos was absorbing stinging single-string solos by B. B. King. Drummer Michael Shrieve was listening to recordings by jazz giants Miles Davis and John Coltrane. Percussionists Carabello and Areas were learning through critically listening to Latin jazz, African drumming, funk, and Jimi Hendrix. The mutual respect for differences in musical taste did not always prevail, however. Additional tension in the band's stylistic "gumbo" came to the fore because promoter Bill Graham insisted on having the group produce short-and-sweet radio-friendly hits.[3]

Graham's insistence on recording "hits" only partially prevailed. Interestingly, only about half of the nine tunes on *Santana*, released in August 1969, were conventional songs with vocals, verses, and choruses. Yet the album hit the Billboard album chart within weeks of its release, with national sales propelling it to the fourth-bestselling album in the United States. Even more impressive, the album remained on the Billboard charts for over two years.

This prevalence of furiously intense Afro-Latin percussion, unprecedented in any previous pop music, fed into the band's public image as wild and cross-cultural. The art Carlos chose for the album cover, a psychedelic lion-man with menacingly open jaws, reinforced that "wildman" image. Les Conklin, the artist, would continue to do eye-catching posters for numerous Bill Graham–sponsored concerts in San Francisco.[4]

By choosing artwork and calligraphy that evoked fierce visionary explorations of consciousness, Carlos gave Graham a way to promote

Santana that differed from other California rock bands considered inspired by drug-catalyzed cosmic visions. Santana's unique racial and cultural mixture, along with its prevalence of members without formal musical academic training or college education, promoted Graham's image of Santana as "the sound of the streets."[5] Santana's hand drummers in 1969 were entirely African American and Latino. Trap drummer Michael Shrieve commented to interviewer Jim McCarthy, "Me and Gregg were curious objects to Carabello and Chepito when we first arrived in the Mission, [but] even though I came from the suburbs and looked like I was twelve, I was around a lot of black folks." Fellow white suburbanite Rolie added, "It was an interesting culture clash joining Santana, meeting the guys in the band; we came from such different backgrounds, nobody understood anybody."[6] By comparison, the two most popular San Francisco psychedelic bands formed prior to Santana, the Grateful Dead and Jefferson Airplane, were entirely Caucasian and middle class, included several members who met in college and one who had extensive formal classical music training.

Additional grit that connected to the band's image was contributed by Rolie and Carlos. Rolie's vocals on the first album are markedly gruff and accusatory in tone, especially on "Evil Ways" and "You Just Don't Care." Carlos conveys street-wise toughness through his stinging electric guitar solos throughout, at times seemingly out-shouting and certainly out-crying Rolie's keyboards while soaring above the roiling percussion section. Carlos crafted a guitar sound that was "fat," thick, searing, and warm, huge and loud enough to cut through a hurricane of percussion, a product both of enormous physical dexterity on the guitar strings and the particular electronic configuration of his guitar and amplifier. For example, the "humbucker" pick-up built into the first Gibson Les Paul guitar he used in the studio was known for producing that thick and bright tone, creating a "brassy" sound Carlos favored.

Since the first album consciously evoked the band's premier at the Woodstock Music Festival through the inclusion of "Soul Sacrifice," a careening instrumental powered by drummer Michael Shrieve, those who were at Woodstock, and the millions who saw the documentary film later released, saw the look on Carlos's face when he played. In an interview for *Guitar Player* magazine, Carlos commented with candor about his facial expressions while playing:

> [P]eople should try to go deeper into the instrument, and transcend its actual construction. To do that, you have to make ugly faces, pucker up your butt, and get to that note.

You need to put different levels of brutal freakin' force behind your playing. The next thing you know, you start getting into a territory that Stevie Ray Vaughan and Jeff Beck inhabit.[7]

CAPTURING ON RECORD ACCURATELY THE SANTANA BAND'S SOUND

Happy to have completed their first album, Carlos was restless and not wholly satisfied with the result. "The first album was soundwise, no; musicwise, yes. . . . By the time we recorded it, it was done very fast with people who had no understanding of the music or how it should be recorded."[8] The album was the result of three weeks sporadically in the recording studio. The session engineers were faced with balancing various Afro-Latin percussionists with a rock-blues guitar, an unprecedented change from how rock albums had been recorded in the 1960s. The percussion sound was murky, but that didn't deter music lovers who appreciated the band's drive and originality. The album sold two million copies in its initial pressing.

Yet this initial burst of success left Carlos restless, anxious for the challenge of the second, more polished studio album, one that would better represent the band's sound. Yet not all band members shared that single-minded purpose. Between the first and second albums, tensions heightened between the view of the band as a completely democratic collective versus the band with Carlos as the undisputed leader.

These tensions were heard in the opening of Santana's second album, *Abraxas*. The opening minute and a half of "Singing Winds, Crying Beasts" was a delicate duet, a call-and-response between Rolie's grandly dramatic opening chords and Carlos's equally dramatic guitar solo laced with sustain. The drummers entered gradually, completely unlike their thunderous immediate presence heard on the first album. This opening signaled a shift in the band's recorded sound from sheer brute percussive force with guitar and keyboard solos to a more textured sound.

This atmospheric tone poem starting *Abraxas* segued into the hit single, "Black Magic Woman/Gypsy Queen," which had originally been recorded in 1968 by Peter Green's Fleetwood Mac. Carlos had been strongly attracted to Green's melodic style from seeing him at Bill Graham's Fillmore. Later, as Carlos entered the international musical spotlight with the first album, he and Green met in both the United States and the United Kingdom to discuss music. In an interview with Ben Fong-Torres, Carlos recalled, "He'd come and hang out with us. He said his band was breaking up. We said, 'You don't have to watch; grab a guitar and play with us.'"[9] Both Green and Carlos were indebted to the style of blues master B. B. King, an approach emphasizing sharply defined, highly melodic, single-string runs, the musical equivalent of sharply articulated verbal jabs.

Santana's version of "Black Magic Woman" differs considerably from that of Green's Fleetwood Mac. The immediate difference is rhythmic. The Fleetwood Mac version utilizes a single drummer playing a steady rock 'n' roll beat. The Santana version is polyrhythmic, with three drummers playing interlocking rhythmic lines, mingling Latin and rock. The introductory guitar solo uses a variety of slides and hammer-ons (meaning that Carlos literally sharply fretted, hammered down the strings of his electric guitar, and then suddenly released them). There is a strong sense of a "crying sound" in this guitar solo increasingly marked by stingingly sustained single-string notes.

After this initial guitar solo, Rolie solos on keyboards, and then sings about "a black magic woman who got me so blind I can't see." There is a less gruff, more understated tone in Rolie's vocal than previously heard on record. Carlos returns with more hypnotic guitar solos after Rolie's vocal. Then the song completely transcends any connection to Peter Green's original by segueing into a rendition of "Gypsy Queen," written by jazz guitarist Gabor Szabo. The Latin drummers suddenly transition from atmospheric colors to majestic, jamming fury. And Carlos rises to the drummers' call by playing a propulsively jazzy solo that suddenly just stops on a sustained single chord before segueing into a Latin music classic written by Tito Puente, "Oye Como Va." "Black Magic Woman" served as a new anthem for the band, reconciling more than ever the various mix of musical styles (rock, blues, Latin) that were synergistic, more than a simple synthesis of otherwise distinctively different styles. Carlos's guitar solos were concise, as succinct as the best radio-friendly rock guitar solos, yet also exotic and jazzy. And the song's subject, a conjuring woman with irresistible supernatural and erotic power, harkened back to one of the most traditionally used images in blues music, the gypsy woman with fortune-telling skills evoked years earlier on the pop record charts by "Gypsy Woman" by Curtis Mayfield and the Impressions.

But "Oye Como Va" (Spanish for "What's happening?" or "How is it going down?") was another surprise for listeners. Perhaps the most surprised was the tune's composer, the man long known in New York's Latin community as the king of mambo, Tito Puente. To shift from the jazzy cover of "Gypsy Queen" to "Oye Como Va" represented a transition back to the band's early Fillmore concerts, where Carlos noticed how the audience danced to the music. Carlos said, "We mixed it up with the African, the Cuban, with Mongo Santamaria, and we started noticing that the hippies were dancing differently."[10] Dancers were swaying their hips sensually, consciously or unconsciously, in gyrations commonly found in African and African American dances. As Carlos characterized the tune, "I thought, this is a song like 'Louie Louie' or 'Guantanamera.' This is a song that when you play it, people are going to get up and dance, and that's it."[11]

Adroitly see-sawing between popular dance rock tunes and jazzy experiments, "Oye Como Va" then transitions into the highly ambitious "Incident at Neshabur," a blend of progressive rock and jazz that seamlessly mixes various time signatures and melodic themes. It was the creation of pianist Alberto Gianquinto, a pianist friend of the band who helped during the recording sessions for Santana's first album. In fact, Gianquinto conceived "Incident at Neshabur" to be showcased on the first album. But its sophisticated atmospheric melodies and tricky rhythmic transitional bridges might have made it a moody oddity in the straightforward, guitar-converses-with-drums feel of Santana's first album. Gianquinto's piano solo on this number effectively integrates with Rolie's increasingly sophisticated keyboard playing on the rest of *Abraxas*.

A marked contrast to the turbulence of "Incident at Neshabur" is "Samba Pa Ti" (meaning "Samba for You"). A meditatively lush and slowly building Latin instrumental with a fervent romantic tone, it was inspired by a quite unromantic situation Carlos saw outside his apartment window: in an alley a guy was blowing saxophone, then drinking booze from a bottle in his back pocket, and then stumbling about trying to decide whether to play more music or get more intoxicated. The melody to "Samba Pa Ti" came to Carlos as he watched this stranger's struggle. The recording marks Carlos's first foray into a traditional form of Brazilian music, one identified with the carnival, and he gently demonstrates tasteful versatility in letting the tune evolve from a slow samba into a moderately speedy and festive tempo. Even without knowing the backstory, it is easy for many listeners to identify with what sounds like a tender and tentative indecisiveness indicative of a divided person gradually transforming into an assured, affirming statement of direction by a person feeling whole, healed.

Abraxas was recorded at Wally Heider's Recording Studio in San Francisco and produced by Fred Catero, who was aware of the dissatisfaction Carlos and some other band members felt about the sound quality of their first album. Catero was tuned into the band both cultur-ally and musically. In an interview, Catero recalls his work during *Abraxas*: "I learned a lot from working on *Abraxas*. I was brought up Spanish and I speak Spanish. You know, if a player says, 'I'm gonna do cascara here' and you don't know what they're saying, that's a big turn off for musicians."[12] Not only was Catero familiar with foundational Latin music patterns like the cascara (a two-bar pattern played in 4/4 time commonly appearing in salsa music), but he appreciated how the band was updating the New York salsa music of the 1950s.

As was true for the first Santana album, cover art enhanced market appeal. In an even more free-form psychedelic style than the first cover, graphic artist Mati Klarwein created a hallucinatory, surrealistic, pop-art mural that put a blood-red angel sitting astride a conga drum apparently giving instruction to a large, African American "earth mother" figure. The "Santana" logo and album name (taken from the name of a goddess in Hermann Hesse's visionary novel *Demian*) seemed suspended in a dreamy atmosphere featuring a larger-than-life sunflower. It is possible that the cover art reflects the type of LSD-induced visions that Carlos had during the summer of 1970. Klarwein acknowledged that he also had experimented with LSD, but denied the drug had any influence on the 1961 painting entitled *Annunication* that Carlos chose for the cover. Interestingly, Carlos included this quote from Hesse's novel in the album's liner notes to illuminate both the cover art and the music:

> We stood before it and began to freeze inside from the exer-tion. We questioned the painting, berated it, made love to it, prayed to it. We called it mother, called it whore and slut, called it our beloved, called it Abraxas.

Hesse's novel was a symbolic story of a young man on a spiritual quest, seeking a level of spiritual understanding deeper than that given to him by his contact with Catholicism as a child. Encounters with var-ious women he loves provide guideposts to achieve this spiritual matu-rity. It might have been a book that young Carlos strongly identified with, given his search for a romantically fulfilling partner and a sense of spiritual grounding at the time *Abraxas* was released.

THE PERILS OF SUCCESS

Abraxas was the bestselling album in the United States for six con-secutive weeks after its release in October 1970. Its overwhelming popularity, with sales so far exceeding the first album, put pressure on the band for increased touring internationally and another album. Success had its perils. Percussionist Michael Carabello had a new roommate on the road, Neal Schon, a fifteen-year-old prodigy on electric guitar. Santana welcomed Schon into the band as a sparring partner on the recommendation of Gregg Rolie and Michael Shrieve. But as Carabello frankly admitted to interviewer Jim McCarthy, "When Neal came out on the road, he'd room with me. We hung out and I taught him some bad habits.... I think what killed us also was we were always on the road—no breaks. I think we were lost for a while."[13] Carlos was even blunter in his comments about this period: "We entered one of the worst periods of my life. Success was getting to be too much. We were trying to make *Santana 3*, but overindulgence in everything available to a successful rock 'n' roller was becoming a problem."[14]

In addition to augmenting the band's identity through welcoming Schon into the core lineup of six, Latin percussionist Thomas "Coke" Escovedo was added to replace the ailing percussionist Chepito Areas. A brain aneurysm kept Areas bedridden in a hospital for six months. Carabello believed that Areas was so essential to the band's success that the group should cease touring and recording until Areas could return. Carlos took strong exception to this position, and asserted his growing leadership of the ground by insisting that Escovedo temporarily take Areas's place. Simmering under this dispute were Carabello and Carlos's differences regarding the band members' increasingly drug-saturated lifestyles. While Carlos felt his own use of psychedelics was justified because he believed that such drugs expanded his musical vision, he was highly critical of heroin and cocaine use by other band members. Along with wild sexual experimentation and alcohol abuse, he saw these activities as leading to a lack of musical commitment and discipline.

In a sense, the arguments Carlos had with Carabello brought to a head a growing sense of alienation with many other band members. This alienation was triggered during the *Abraxas* recording sessions, as Carlos informed biographer Marc Shapiro, "I remember I started to pull rank on the band.... In the past, things had been very democratic. But the band did not want the songs 'Oye Como Va' and 'Samba Pa Ti' on the record. They said it didn't sound like Santana. We went back and forth a long time before I finally said, 'Either these two songs go on the album or you go find another guitar player.'"[15] Although this tactic worked for Carlos during the *Abraxas* sessions, it would fail when Carlos tried it again as a way to get Carabello out of the group. The band went on tour for two weeks without Carlos.

One way to comprehend why tensions between Carlos and the other band members heated up so intensely after *Abraxas* is to place the band's conflicts within the context of what had happened to the Bay Area's countercultural scene at the start of the 1970s. When Carlos began putting together a band in the 1960s, there was among a number of the already established San Francisco rock bands, like Jefferson Airplane and the Grateful Dead, a belief in music as a unifying force that could catalyze peace and love. This notion of members of a musical group unselfishly relating to one another, producing music that could eventually harmonize the world, was held by many artists and intellectuals in the Bay Area during the sixties. It was a time when many artists believed in consciousness-altering music (the more scholarly label for "psychedelic music") as a type of religion promising redemption, if not salvation. A band without an obvious leader was a utopian experiment in musical democracy—and utopian aspirations were in the air throughout much of the sixties, crowned by the spectacular success of the Woodstock Musical Festival in 1969.

The "peace and love" ethos impacted rock bands far from San Francisco. For example, lead vocalist for the Rolling Stones Mick Jagger told a reporter before the band's 1969 American tour, "It's creating a sort of a microcosmic society.... It sets an example to the rest of America, as to how one can behave in nice gatherings."[16] But the atmosphere that largely permeated the Woodstock Festival was short-lived, a transformation that the Santana band witnessed first-hand when they played the Altamont Music Festival at the end of 1969. The concert was an ill-conceived event at a northern California racetrack, in which Hell's Angels motorcycle gang members were hired to act as security guards. One concertgoer was killed and several injured. The Santana band, opening for the Rolling Stones, ended their set after only four songs—with one interrupted by Hell's Angels running across the stage through their ranks. Both the Santana band and the Rolling Stones were powerless to stop the violence. The impact of this event reverberated throughout the early 1970s since the Altamont concert was recorded in part in a highly popular documentary film, *Gimme Shelter*, directed by brothers Albert and David Maysles and Charlotte Zwerin. Santana's performance was not included in the documentary.

THE MAKING OF THE THIRD SANTANA ALBUM

Peacefulness was also not the prevailing feeling when the Santana band began recording its third album at a new Columbia recording studio in San Francisco. Guest percussionist Thomas "Coke" Escovedo, although he was accepted by the band as a temporary replacement for Chepito Areas, was resented by some band members for allegedly influencing the musical decisions Carlos made. Debates also raged regarding using a guest horn section, in this case, the Tower of Power, on the tune "Everyone's Everything." This was ironic, given the fact that the album's opening, full-bore, polyrhythmic instrumental, "Batuka," was presented on the *Bell Telephone TV Hour* in which the band was integrated with the entire Los Angles Philharmonic, their brass and woodwind sections augmenting the group with more than triple the number of horn players Tower of Power used.[17] On the one hand, Tower of Power was an emergent Bay Area band in need of greater national exposure, and Carlos had a penchant for helping young local musicians who were ambitious and disciplined. On the other hand, Santana was original in the history of U.S. Latin music at that time for substituting electric guitar and keyboard for the traditional brass instrumentation found in mambo and salsa bands.

And the band was also faced with the challenge of how to integrate Neal Schon's guitar as a second guitar voice in a band so heavily percussive and so dominated by a single guitarist's style. Adding fuel to the tension in the recording studio was some musicians' ongoing drug abuse, which didn't promote clear collective reasoning about musical focus. Ironically, the tune that Escovedo and Carabello brought to the session, "No One to Depend On," a partial adaptation of a Willie Bobo composition, "Spanish Grease," recorded years earlier by Bobo, could have been the band's anthem in 1971.

Yet the resulting album turned out to a highly cohesive product, arguably as fine an achievement as *Abraxas*. The opening selection, "Batuka," immediately sets the recording apart from *Abraxas* by opening with a thundering, polyrhythmic choir of drummers preparing the way for the guitarists. The interaction between Carlos and Schon is like a dialogue between highly competitive, but ultimately harmonious brothers. There is an exciting call-and-response dynamic present throughout the album, with Schon's guitar solos marked by spine-tingling treble-note flurries and the frequent use of a wah-wah pedal. Carlos's solos have his characteristic blend of blues cries, strong Latin dance rhythms, and lush Latin melodies. Interestingly, when the guitarists play in unison, the thickening of the band's electric guitar sound contributes to the appreciation of how guitars were taking the place of brass dominant in salsa bands.

The furious rhythmic workout suggested by "Batuka" establishes a feel for the album, prosaically titled *Santana III*, and echoes through other breakneck instrumentals that are highpoints, "Toussaint L'Overture," a moody tone poem with structural parallels to "Incident at Nushbur" on *Abraxas*, "Jungle Strut," and "Para Los Rumberos," the band's second cover of a Tito Puente Latin music classic. "Jungle Strut" appeared on Gene Ammons' "Brother Jug" album two years earlier and seems to reflect the veteran jazz saxophonist's desire to reach a larger pop music audience. Ammons added a funky wah-wah guitar to the arrangement of his jazz tune, making it an apt for the band to cover. Leaving the wah-wah guitar part to Schon, Carlos delivers some blisteringly jazzy riffs in counterpoint to Schon's funk-rock effects. Santana's third album is a distillation of the rhythmic fury of their first album with the polished musicianship of their second. The guest horns adds a little color in the case of "Everybody's Everything" that rides on Rolie's soul-flavored vocal. The effectiveness of the added horns is debatable since Carlos and Schon enter the number only after Rolie, the rhythm section and horns have their say for half the song's duration. Listeners might find Gregg Rolie's vocal, James Brown–like injunction of "Get Down!" more memorable than many other facets of the tune, though Carlos adds a guitar solo uncannily echoing Rolie's vocal inflections. A sharper integration of the horn into the band's sound comes from trumpeter Luis Gasca on "Para Los Rumberos." His soaring, high-resister flourishes add spice to the Puente cover. Gasca, a friend of Carlos, had a history of performing jazz and Latin music from the 1950s on with stars like Count Basie and Tito Puente. After the sessions for *Santana III* concluded in June 1971, most of the band recorded with Gasca on his eponymously titled solo album for the Blue Thumb label.

Another offshoot of the *Santana III* recording experience was playing at the closing concert for the Fillmore West, Bill Graham's venue, honoring the band's musical mentor and financial advisor. As was the case with the Woodstock Festival, the band's performance was a capstone of the event, though a complete commercially available recording only was made available a quarter century later. *Santana III* was met with critical praise and dazzling sales. It assumed the number 1 spot on the Billboard sales chart shortly after its release. And the song "Everything's Coming Our Way," appearing near the album's close, could have been logically interpreted as a foreshadowing of more fulfilling times for the band to come. But *Santana III* was also the swan song of the original band that enthralled fans at Woodstock.

Central to the breakup of the band was the miscommunication among musicians worsened by drug abuse. As Gregg Rolie said, "The third album had everything on it; I think the band jelled well. When the music didn't jell, our communication wasn't there." Neal Schon seconded Rolie's comment to McCarthy but made his memory of the time more specific. "The original band was a monster in its own right. Looking at it now, had everyone not been so high, we might have weathered it."[18]

Michael Carabello summed up the time by describing how drugs were "free flow then" and helped—or gave band members the illusion of being helped through the stresses of highly intensive touring.[19]

Mind-altering drugs were easily available to Santana's members, and there was a tacit understanding that the drugs could be handled without bizarre consequences in the conventional world. The band members quickly forgot their initial hassles during the start of the recording session of *Santana III* when, under the influence, band members damaged a brand-new recording studio. Contributing to the easy rationalization for destructive behavior was the perception that Bay Area culture had always been forgiving of bizarre public behavior. It was part and parcel of San Francisco's historic reputation of tolerating forms of bohemian excess. But what made Santana musicians unique was that they had an extraordinary amount of disposable income to spend on drugs. The sister of bassist David Brown recalled her shock to Jim McCarthy when she discovered that her brother had a $250-a-day drug habit.[20] A casual high from smoking marijuana at the time would have cost a few dollars. But the cocaine high that many Santana musicians commonly experienced could cost hundreds of dollars.

Matters worsened, ironically, when the band had a meeting at Gregg Rolie's house in Mill Valley to try to save themselves from drug abuse. According to Rolie's version of the meeting, everyone except Carlos agreed to curb his drug and alcohol problem. Carlos defended his right to use LSD anytime. To make matters worse, those managing the touring and financial affairs of the band were often abusing drugs themselves.[21]

Twenty-one-year-old millionaires have never been known for sound financial judgment and psychological maturity. Their sudden fame and fortune carried with it an illusion of grandiose power in the outer world. Both cocaine (everyone but Carlos's favorite drug apparently) and LSD (Carlos's alleged drug of choice) blur boundaries between what is a person's real self and everything else in the world. Blurred boundaries of personal responsibility quickly destroyed the communal air of respect that once permeated the band.

No greater proof that the cohesive Santana band of 1969 to 1971 was gone forever was the next album, entitled *Carlos Santana & Buddy Miles Live!* The title clearly announced that this was a showcase for

Carlos even though there were far fewer of his guitar solos on this 1972 live concert from Hawaii than on the previous Santana albums. The alliance with drummer and vocalist Buddy Miles was a shrewd commercial move on Carlos's part since Miles was a well-recognized drummer for guitar-titan Jimi Hendrix. In 1972, only two years after Hendrix's death, any music associated with him had cachet in terms of sales. But Carlos's alliance with Miles was also a musical adventure in terms of departing from Latin music and moving in the direction of jazzy funk and mainstream rock.

Only guitarist Neal Schon and percussionists Michael Carabello and Coke Escovedo were band holdovers from *Santana III*. The remaining players were either connected with Buddy Miles or Bay Area studio musicians. The concert was recorded inside a Hawaiian volcanic crater, once again a nod to the Jimi Hendrix legacy since one of the final Hendrix concerts, documented on the *Rainbow Bridge* film, was also performed at a Hawaiian volcano. The music on the album was an odd assortment of funk riffs from Miles and a few free jazz jams that resembled a rock band attempting to play the avant-garde jazz of Pharoah Sanders. Half of the album was a 25-minute jam loosely based on a song by jazz vocalist Leon Thomas, who did perform with Pharoah Sanders and who later joined the new Santana band. Rumors abounded after the album's release that Carlos was unhappy with the album. Although it was panned by most musical critics, it sold remarkably well. And the album's few moments of Carlos's jazzy improvisational guitar soloing was a portent of what the next evolution of his band would sound like.

NOTES

1. Ben Fong-Torres, liner notes for CD booklet for 1998 reissue of *Santana* CD.

2. Steve Heilig, "The World of Carlos Santana," *The Beat* 19, no. 1 (2000): 43.

3. Fong-Torres, *Santana* reissue CD booklet.

4. Lee Conklin's print for the album cover continues to be available through the artist who resides in Columbia, California.

5. Graham is heard introducing Santana this way on the *Fillmore: The Last Days* CD box set.

6. Jim McCarthy with Ron Sansoe, with foreword by Carlos Santana, *Voices of Latin Rock: The People and Events That Created This Sound* (Milwaukee: Hal Leonard Corporation, 2004), 35.

7. Darrin Fox, "Carlos Santana Spreads the Gospel of Tone," *Guitar Player*, May 2005, http://www.guitarplayer.com/article/carlos-santana-spreads/May-05/8870.

8. McCarthy with Sansoe, *Voices of Latin Rock*, 57.

9. Ben Fong-Torres, liner notes written for the thirtieth anniversary CD reissue of *Abraxas*.

10. Heilig, "World of Carlos Santana," 44.

11. Fong-Torres, liner notes for *Abraxas* reissue.

12. McCarthy with Sansoe, *Voices of Latin Rock*, 63.

13. Ibid., 95.

14. Ibid.

15. Marc Shapiro, *Carlos Santana: Back on Top* (New York: St. Martin's Griffin, 2002), 106.

16. Philip Norman, *Sympathy for the Devil: The Rolling Stones Story* (New York: Simon and Schuster, 1984), 329.

17. A video of the performance is available at http://www.facebook.com/video/video.php?v=1003792211724, in which the song is misidentified as "Jungle Strut" and the conductor of the Los Angeles Philharmonic is identified alternately as Leonard Bernstein and Zehta. Rolie in the liner notes to the album reissue identified Leonard Bernstein as the arranger.

18. McCarthy with Sansoe, *Voices of Latin Rock*, 93.

19. Ibid., 95.

20. Ibid, 100.

21. The chapter entitled "No One to Depend On" (95–106) in ibid., gives a comprehensive overview of key problems the band had with drug abuse.

Chapter 4

TRYING ON THE SPIRIT OF JAZZ

Carlos had heard jazz before ever dreaming of living in the United States and forming his own band. He recalled in one interview his father playing guitar runs that were reminiscent of Django Reinhardt and big band swing evocative of Duke Ellington.[1] But Carlos did not have the emotional involvement with jazz that marked his encounter with the blues until he began to hear jazz bands in concert at Bill Graham's Fillmore auditorium in 1966. Graham's musical taste ensured an unusually eclectic blend of jazz, Latin, and rock music, reflecting his awareness that rock music was becoming progressively more complex and open to a large range of diverse musical styles.

Carlos had always taken pleasure in hearing live improvised music. A large inspiration for the original formation of the Santana band was the various drum groups that informally jammed for hours in Bay Area parks. Carlos was also taken with the blues jams popularized by the Paul Butterfield Blues Band, another Graham favorite.

Of the jazz performers Carlos heard at the Fillmore, Gabor Szabo, who opened for the jazz saxophonist Charles Lloyd, had the most immediate and crucial influence. Before hearing Szabo, Carlos described in a documentary film what his state of mind was. "When I came to America, most of my guitar language was derived from B. B. King, Freddie King, and Albert King.... He [Szabo] was my freeway exit out from B. B. King."[2] Szabo, who has remained a footnote, if mentioned at all, in most jazz history books, influenced Carlos by offering "a new world of possibilities on guitar." These included the appropriation of seemingly trite pop melodies (Sonny and Cher's "Bang Bang" and "The Beat Goes On") as the melodic basis of jazzy improvisation, the use of unusual guitar tunings and picking styles evocative of both Latin and Asian musical traditions (particularly Indian), a lyrical singing tone with many notes held for long measures, and a tamed but emotionally riveting use of guitar feedback resembling the drone tone in Indian ragas. First as the guitarist in Chico Hamilton's jazz group, then as leader of his own group, Szabo had an immigrant's apprenticeship as a young man to the United States, an affinity Carlos recognized, in that Szabo had to arduously win what he called "the right to my own style."[3]

"Gypsy Queen" was an original composition that Carlos heard on Szabo's 1966 *Spellbinder* album, one inspired by the experiences Szabo had as a young child seeing wild gypsy dances at night in the cornfields of his native Hungary. "These occasions, always so wildly romantic, mystical, and a little fearful, made a deep impression on me," wrote Szabo in his album's liner notes. The words "romantic," "mystical," and "fearful" could just as accurately describe the emotional guitar style that evolved into Carlos's. And Szabo's "Gypsy Queen" became one of the high points of Santana's *Abraxas* album.

Another jazz guitarist whom Carlos heard at The Fillmore was Bola Sete, a transplanted Brazilian who joined the popular Bay Area jazz group led by pianist Vince Guaraldi. Carlos credited Sete, yet another jazz figure marginalized in conventional jazz histories, as an "Afro-Brazilian Segovia" who taught him how "to listen to inner music … beyond the self." Also like Szabo, Sete was willing to dust off tawdry pop melodies ("A Taste of Honey," "The Girl from Ipanema") and use them as the basis for refreshing musical reinterpretations through creative improvisation. Sete had a flair for performing Afro-Latin dance rhythms on guitar, a clear influence on Carlos's guitar playing. But unlike Szabo, Sete depended on no electronic embellishment of his sounds, a reminder to Carlos of the expressive range of a purely acoustic guitar, an instrument he would practice with often.

As significant as these jazz guitarists were in terms of Carlos developing a distinctive sound, far more significant in terms of introducing a "big picture" of jazz to Carlos was drummer Michael Shrieve. Carlos often credited Shrieve with catalyzing his lifetime interest in the music of saxophonist John Coltrane and trumpeter Miles Davis. The acquaintance with Davis's recordings led to direct contact, and a lasting friendship, with the trumpeter. Since Bill Graham also loved Miles Davis's work, he booked Davis to play at the Fillmore with the cream of the Bay Area's more experimental and musically eclectic rock bands.

Soon Santana was playing on the same date with Miles Davis. And the timing was fortunate for both musicians.

Miles Davis in the late 1960s was radically altering his musical approach and increasingly incorporating rock instrumentation and riffs into his jazz, culminating with the hit albums *In a Silent Way* and *Bitches Brew*, which set a watermark for the mix of jazz and rock that began to be known as "Fusion." With *Bitches Brew* Miles also experimented with the cyclic and danceable rhythms of funk, finding inspiration from bands like Sly and the Family Stone and Funkadelic. With the music of jazz-rock by Miles Davis likely in his mind when he entered the recording studio in the summer of 1972, Carlos began working on *Caravanserai* with the newly configured Santana band. Douglas Rauch had replaced David Brown on bass. A former Gabor Szabo keyboardist, Tom Coster, performed on a number of selections when the increasingly estranged Gregg Rolie felt disconnected from Carlos's new compositions. And percussionist Armando Peraza, a veteran player who had recorded with jazz masters Charlie Parker and Art Blakey, was added to the rhythm section.

In spite of these major personnel shifts, the new incarnation of Santana still had times of embodying the original group sound, particularly as on *Santana III*. This was most evident on "Song of the Wind," an instrumental with an intensely fiery dialogue of sharply etched, electric guitar solos between Carlos and Neal Schon that suggested a father and son arguing passionately and then reconciling. But much was also remarkably different. Particularly telling was the choice of a cover tune, far removed from the Latin funk and bluesy rock of earlier Santana albums. Carlos and Shrieve tackled the ambitious and internationally popular Brazilian pop composer Tom Jobim and put their unmistakably musical fingerprints on the Afro-Brazilian composition "Stone Flower." This was the first major recorded foray Carlos made into Brazilian music, although "Samba Pa Ti" touched upon samba rhythms intermingled with Latin melodies, and he would continue to mine this musical heritage in future albums. Jobim had been a major vehicle for significant jazz artists like Stan Getz; by tackling Jobim, Carlos was taking another step in the direction of cosmopolitan jazz.

While Carlos was elated to experiment in a jazz-rock direction with his new band, the recording company executives at Columbia Record's New York offices were far from delighted. The company expressed their displeasure to Carlos for the first—but far from the last—time in terms of their fears that Carlos was pursuing a commercially moribund direction. And for far from the last time, Carlos heatedly informed the executives that he intended to remain faithful to his evolving musical vision that was carrying him away from purely Latin-tinged rock into a Latin-tinged, rock-jazz hybrid. As Carlos explained to an interviewer in response to the question, "Can you point to an album of yours as a watershed moment in your development as a player?":

> There were two: *Caravanserai* and *Welcome*. At that time, I felt my whole existence pulled toward John Coltrane. I remember going to the record company and telling them, "I know what you want, but I can't give it to you because I don't hear it." I knew I would pay the price by not selling a ton of records, but I didn't care.[4]

The opening of *Caravanserai* evolves into the dreamy atmosphere of "Singing Winds, Crying Beasts" opening the *Abraxas* album. But a curious difference is that the only guitarist heard on the tune is Neal Schon, with Carlos content to contribute percussion. Most distinctive is the harsh throaty saxophone solo by guest artist Hadley Caliman in counterpoint to what sounds like cicadas. Carlos returns full-force on the next instrumental, "Waves Within," a rock-jazz fusion instrumental, and maintains the position of sole lead guitar player on half of the album's tunes.

Both Carlos's guitar playing and the band sound on *Caravanserai* represent a considerable advance in refinement and sophistication from the previous albums. And for Carlos this musical advance was hard won, as he informed music journalist Marc Shapiro: "I was moving into the unknown. I couldn't read music and I was working with advanced musicians who were well into jazz."[5]

Another source of creative tension was the immanent departure of Gregg Rolie and Neal Schon to form the band Journey. Carlos had been a close mentor to the teenage Schon and had enjoyed having a sparring partner on guitar. "Song of the Wind" was both a highwater mark for their collaboration on guitar and a swan song. Rolie had been with Carlos from the beginning of the Santana band. So while their parting was less than amicable, Carlos could not forget the way they had banded together at Woodstock, on their first three albums, and on international tour. Out of these forces came an album that won both critical acclaim for Carlos and, to the surprise of record company executives, robust if not spectacular sales.

Another indicator of Carlos's evolution toward jazz was the addition of an acoustic bassist, Tom Rutley, who plays in tandem with electric bassist Rauch on "All the Love of the Universe." Dual bassists had been used by jazz revolutionaries John Coltrane, Ornette Coleman, and Miles Davis, and created a densely complex rhythmic foundation, one Carlos found inspirational. Another offbeat instrumental pairing Carlos used effectively is heard on "La Fuente Del Ritmo," where James Mingo Lewis on acoustic piano plays contrasting lines to Tom Coster's electric piano. These varieties of instrumental doubling are best heard on the album's final three instrumentals, "Stone Flower," "La Fuente Del Ritmo," and "Every Step of the Way." Each can be heard as a tour de force of rapidly unfolding rhythmic fury and harmonic complexity. This was the first Santana album that defied the commercial expectation that a radio-friendly hit single could be cherrypicked from the album. *Caravanserai* seemed to some listeners as one long suite, a concept album where individual selections matter less than a unitary instrumental statement.

The months following the completion of *Caravanserai* brought together a series of highly satisfying musical as well as spiritual connections for Carlos. At the suggestion of Columbia Records executive Clive Davis, Carlos recorded with John McLaughlin, an English jazz guitarist whose playing with Miles Davis Carlos had keenly appreciated. Miles Davis was so taken by McLaughlin's guitar playing that he even titled a key composition on *Bitches Brew* simply "John McLaughlin." McLaughlin left Davis and became the leader of a pioneering jazz fusion band, the Mahavishnu Orchestra, which Carlos loved. In fact, Deborah Santana recalled that during their courtship, one of the albums Carlos most expressed enthusiasm about was the Mahavishnu Orchestra's *Birds of Fire*.[6] McLaughlin, a few years older than Carlos, and most conversant with the jazz scene, would take Neal Schon's place in terms of being a guitar partner, pushing Carlos into new heights of improvised expression. And while Michael Shrieve could introduce Carlos to Coltrane and Miles Davis through recordings, McLaughlin had been in the recording studio and concert stage with major American and European experimental jazz artists, including vibraphonist Karl Berger, bassist Dave Holland, and saxophonist John Surman. He also recorded an album of jazz and a heavy rock undertow, *Devotion*, with drummer Buddy Miles, shortly before Carlos joined forced with the drummer for the live album marking the end of the original Santana band.

But McLaughlin's role in Carlos's life in 1972 was more than just musical. McLaughlin had come under the spell of a spiritual teacher, Sri Chinmoy, and encouraged Carlos to join him in that devotion to the Indian guru. Chinmoy (1927–2007) offered to both McLaughlin and Carlos a disciplined spiritual path that forbad the use of drugs and alcohol and encouraged music and poetry as expressions of thankfulness to the Divine. Although Carlos would later come to strongly disavow his connection with Chinmoy's spiritual path, there was little question that it helped catalyze his musical creativity in the early 1970s.

In addition to Chinmoy's spiritual perspective, Carlos brought to his collaboration with McLaughlin veneration for the jazz tenor saxophonist John Coltrane. Coltrane had fused his own eclectic sense of Eastern and Western spirituality into A Love Supreme, a musical masterpiece both Carlos and McLaughlin knew well. A Love Supreme would have been an ambitious project for the most sophisticated jazz veteran since Coltrane's saxophone solos ranged from soft and soothing whispers to screamingly ecstatic, prayer-like choruses. In crafting their own version of Coltrane's most famous spiritually charged album, Carlos and McLaughlin traded off inspired electric guitar solos that took advantage of the differences in their playing styles. McLaughlin was a loquacious player, rattling off pelting showers of notes at supersonic speed, a guitar parallel to the piano style of jazz pianist Art Tatum. Carlos played more sparsely and was never one to dazzle purely through speedy execution of riffs. He had a deeply rooted love for anchoring embellishment upon simple melodies while McLaughlin was more driven to explore free jazz unshackled from conventional melodic song. Carlos's background in B. B. King never left him, meaning that he wanted as few, deeply felt, guitar notes to linger in a listener's mind. Carlos's and McLaughlin's opposing guitar styles meshed together particularly well on the two Coltrane compositions on the Love Devotion Surrender album, "A Love Supreme" and "Naima," the latter a gentle love song Coltrane wrote in honor of his first wife. Carlos engaged in a guitar collaboration at this point quite different from those of other major rock guitarists like Eric Clapton and Jeff Beck. By not trying to outdo McLaughlin in speed and complexity, and maintaining the passionate melodic integrity of his own style, Carlos avoided the superstar "cutting contest" competitiveness that often marred recorded meetings of guitar giants in the 1970s.

Helping the guitar collaboration were Santana band members Michael Shrieve on drums, Doug Rauch on bass, and Armando Peraza on congas. Yet another cohering musical presence was organist Larry Young, who had a distinguished career in both a jazz-fusion group led by ex–Miles Davis drummer Tony Williams and playing briefly in a progressive rock session with Jimi Hendrix. Young seemed to carefully thread his way between the two blazing guitars, adding unexpected ethereal colors to the proceedings.

The cover photograph, credited to "Ashok," was likely a shock to those who recalled how Carlos looked on stage from 1969 to 1971. His long hair was carefully cropped. His jeans and tie-dyed shirts were also gone. Instead, he appeared in a white linen suit alongside the similarly clad McLaughlin. The third person in the photograph was their guru, Sri Chinmoy. The overt nature of this spiritual devotion by the guitarists brought a wave of cynical comments by the music press. Most scathing was this quip by Robert Christgau, a long-time critic for the *Village Voice*, about the album cover photograph:

> Two of them are dressed in white and have their hands folded—one grinning like Alfred E. Neuman, the other looking like he's about to have a Supreme Court case named after him: solemn, his wrists ready for the cuffs. In between, a man in an orange ski jacket and red pants with one white sock seems to have caught his tongue on his lower lip. He looks like the yoga coach at a fashionable lunatic asylum. Guess which one is Sri Chinmoy?[7]

Carlos was the one Christgau identified as looking like a candidate for a Supreme Court case named after him. Interestingly, the 2003 CD reissue has Chinmoy's portrait edited out of the photograph, reflecting, one speculates, the distance the guitarists wanted to put between themselves and their former guru.

But Chinmoy's impact on Carlos in 1972 was sweeping. It extended to having his name changed by Chinmoy to "Devadip" (meaning "the light of the lamp of God") so that Carlos began releasing his albums under that name. He also began to set several of Chinmoy's thousands of poems and songs to music and continued along the commercially and artistically risky path of merging his roots in rock music with his newfound appreciation of daringly improvisatory jazz.

Carlos's life changed significantly in 1973. He married Deborah King, daughter of respected R&B guitarist Saunders King. According to Deborah Santana's memoir, *Space Between the Stars*, she and Carlos began their romance after she had broken off being Sly Stone's girlfriend.[8] Carlos was contending with a breakup of his own when they met, though not of the romantic kind. The original Santana band had broken up, with only Michael Shrieve and Gregg Rolie remaining. Deborah and Carlos immediately found a connection in their love of

music and their wish to adopt lifestyles infused with a blending of Eastern and Western spirituality. A particular shared interest was Indian
philosophy, including meditation and yoga, which led them into the
spiritual community established by Sri Chinmoy. They also both had
fathers who were life-long professional musicians. They understood the
sacrifices spouses and other family members often had to make when
one family member had a life in the music business. And they also
understood the satisfaction derived from a life of bringing joy into people's lives through music.

Musically Carlos began the year leading his band on an international
tour that was interrupted during the spring long enough to record a new
album. *Welcome* represented for Carlos an even deeper probe into jazz
than *Caravanserai*. He enlisted Leon Thomas, a highly respected jazz vocalist who had performed both with Count Basie's big band and the
avant-garde band of tenor saxophonist Pharoah Sanders. To play with a
member of the Sanders band further cemented the musical and spiritual
connection Carlos felt to John Coltrane. Sanders and Coltrane had performed in concert and recorded together often between 1965 and Coltrane's death in 1967. Other veteran jazz musicians brought into the
studio included the Brazilian vocalist Flora Purim and reed player Joe
Farrell. And as a code to their pairing on *Love Devotion Surrender*, John
McLaughlin was on hand to improvise with Carlos on "Flame-sky."

The ambitiousness of the album is apparent from the opening lush
melody, "Going Home," an African American folksong at the melodic
center of Antonin Dvořák's *New World Symphony*, stated by the twin
synthesizers of Tom Coster and Richard Kermode, former keyboardist
in Malo, a Latin rock band led by Jorge Santana, Carlos's younger
brother. Drummer Michael Shrieve adds a spectacular bed of resound-
ing rhythms on drums with cascading cymbal play, and Carlos joins
Armando Peraza on percussion. The impact is majestic and adventure-
some, a feeling maintained throughout the album. Highlights include
"Samba de Sausalito," another sign of the interest Carlos was taking in
Afro-Brazilian music, and a devout cover of John Coltrane's "Welcome"
that rousingly concluded the album.

And as was the case with *Caravanserai*, the Columbia Records marketing department was not certain about the album's commercial
appeal. Curiously, it took 27 years before the company rereleased *Welcome* in a compact-disc format. But another recording the Santana
band made in 1973, *Lotus*, suffered an even more ignoble fate.

After completing *Welcome*, the band continued international touring, and performed in July 1973 at Osaka Koseinenkin Hall in Japan.

The concert was recorded and showcased nearly the same band personnel as on *Welcome*, minus Joe Farrell and Flora Purim. Santana fans eagerly anticipated its release since it was the Santana's band first live recording, the earlier "live" collaboration with Buddy Miles being a gathering of musicians from various bands. A triple-LP, limited-edition box set was offered for sale in Japan. It was only available to the band's North American fans as an extremely expensive and difficult to obtain import. *Lotus* would not be reissued on compact disc in North America until 1991. An immediate impression this first live album indicates was that Carlos chose to speak to his audience, unlike many other rock stars, entirely through his music. The lack of any comments by any band members, along with an audio mix that disclosed only faint audience applause, let some Santana fans to gossip that it was not a "real" live album at all, although plentiful evidence to the contrary exists.

The album, opening with a rootsy samba march identified with percussion, consists mainly of long instrumentals, with a handful of Santana favorites from the band's first albums, "Black Magic Woman/Gypsy Queen," "Samba Pa Ti," and "Incident at Neshabur," the tune drawn into a 15-minute frenzied exercise in intelligent group improvisation. Of note is a guitar solo that makes explicit Carlos's musical and spiritual communion with John Coltrane. Parts of two of Coltrane's most popular recordings, "My Favorite Things" and "Afro Blue," are directly though fleetingly quoted, note for note. "Gypsy Queen" and "Samba De Sausalito" lack the polish of their studio versions, both victims of the lack of studio recording conditions for maximal clarity. The album centrally reflects the daringly experimental spirit that keyboardist Tom Coster, matched with new keyboardist Richard Kermode, and Carlos brought to their world tour. Coster seems particularly taken by experimenting with dramatic "sci-fi"-type sounds (rocket-engine thrusts, robotic trills) he could coax from his electronic keyboards. *Lotus* also gives drummer Michael Shrieve his first recorded opportunity to perform a long (10-minute) drum solo, his only extended solo with Carlos on record. It also is a valuable recording of vocalist Leon Thomas, who would leave the band upon the tour's completion and return to a solo career within avant-garde jazz.

Of the scores of vocalists Carlos has utilized over the years, Thomas was arguably the most unique, bringing to the band a throaty type of yodel that was a clever adaptation of the singing style of the Mbuti pygmies of the Ituri rainforest in Africa. His demonstrations of this otherworldly singing style on "When I Look Into Your Eyes" on *Welcome* and "Mr. Udo" on *Lotus* very much conjured the kind of African-flavored cosmic spirituality that Carlos was aiming for in his guitar work and band sound.

The next internationally available album from Santana was *Borboletta*, a studio production from 1974. This was a surprise after the jazzy trilogy of *Caravanserai, Welcome,* and *Lotus* (which seemed a consolation and expansion upon the first two in the trilogy). Carlos invited Flora Purim back along with her husband, the percussionist Airto Moreira. This signaled that the Afro-Brazilian music Carlos had recorded on *Welcome* was more than just a passing fancy. Also added to the band was Jules Broussard, a Bay Area jazz saxophonist who was the most sophisticated saxophonist to play with Carlos up to this point. The highly esteemed jazz-rock bassist Stanley Clarke, a member of pianist Chick Corea's *Return to Forever* fusion band, also appears on a number of tunes. While less musically daring than *Caravanserai, Welcome,* and *Lotus, Borboletta* offers a happily upbeat mix of Afro-Brazilian and funk rhythms. Song lyrics, almost entirely penned by Carlos, are spiritual exhortations and sermons in the key of Chinmoy. Songs include "Life Is New," "One with the Sun," and "Practice What You Preach." Less marked by long instrumental jams that characterized his three previous albums, *Borboletta* is perhaps Carlos's attempt to create a jazz rock music that would still be immensely radio friendly. The upbeat tone of many of the songs might have reflected the pride of fatherhood since that year his wife gave birth to their first child, Salvador.

If *Borboletta* represents more of a commercially appealing form of jazzy Brazilian music, *Illuminations,* a recorded collaboration that same year with Alice Coltrane, the widow of John Coltrane and an avant-garde harpist and keyboardist, was apparently a project unconnected to widespread commercial appeal. It offered Carlos in a setting largely devoid of polyrhythmic drumming, his signature rhythmic foundation until this time. Instead, a 16-piece string orchestra joined by organ and piano swirls around harp arpeggios by Alice Coltrane, interlaced with pensive and restrained melodic guitar solos by Carlos. Some listeners felt that it was an album of "New Age" music, spiritually tinged mood music intended primarily for metaphysical meditation rather than for sensual musical enjoyment or dancing. Coltrane shared a fervent, Indian-flavored spirituality with Carlos so their collaboration unsurprisingly reflects the devotional focus of both musicians. Most shocking to Carlos's fans was the complete absence of Latin percussion on three of the album's four lengthy compositions. When Latin percussion was included on "Angel of Sunlight," conga drummer Armando Peraza was joined by the tabla (Indian drum) player Phil Ford in a tune that oscillates between Indian raga (then identified in countercultural circles with sitarist Ravi Shankar) and Latin jazz jam.

It was also not surprising to Columbia records that sales of *Illuminations* were the most disappointing of any solo or band effort by Carlos to that date. Although Carlos could feel encouraged with some positive reviews by jazz critics in prestigious magazines like *Downbeat*, he was aware by the end of 1974 that his massive international fan base was beginning to slightly diminish.

Carlos had complex and contradictory feelings about his musical identity at the time of these albums. He gave interviews in which he blamed Columbia Records for failing to promote his jazzier, more experimental albums. But he had not publicly declared himself a jazz musician rather than a pop and rock musician. And he had strayed far from the cornerstones of his guitar styles, the blues and Afro-Latin rhythms. Jazz bassist Reggie Workman, who had recorded with John Coltrane, chastised Carlos during a recording session for *Illuminations* in words that likely touched Carlos to the quick: "'You ought to look at what you're doing,' Workman sharply spoke. 'A lot of people look up to you. It's not so important, getting into Coltrane. Get into yourself.'"[9]

Further, everyone acquainted with Carlos in 1974 understood that Bill Graham, a kind of musical as well as financial "father figure" to Carlos, was unhappy with the commercially unsuccessful jazz-rock spiritual adventures Carlos was recording. It was Graham who insisted at the very beginning of the first Santana band that Carlos and crew go for radio-friendly songs. That was why Graham brought Willie Bobo's "Evil Ways" to the band's attention and rejoiced when "Black Magic Woman" hit the charts. To what degree Carlos felt free to argue about his musical direction, no one knows for certain. Carlos has always been cautious in voicing public criticism about the man who did so much to launch his career at the Woodstock Music Festival. But Graham's friends and detractors agree that Graham was a hard person to argue with.

Perhaps Carlos, who had grown accustomed to mass fan adoration, struggled with the desire to keep that adoration while at the same time wanting to educate his fans to be more accepting of his jazzier and more spiritual direction. Jazz has never been a music that attracts mass adoring audiences. Jazz recordings call for longer attention spans than typical rock songs and rarely invite conventional dancing. Jazz transcends the tendency toward formulaic, two or three chord "changes" common to rock. And finally, jazz stars never remotely make the kind of money Carlos was making when he was playing music easily categorized as "rock." Whatever was passing through his mind at the end of

1974, we do know that his next album two years later marked a return to his earlier musical roots.

NOTES

1. Marc Shapiro, *Carlos Santana: Back on Top* (New York: St. Martin's Griffin, 2002), 14.

2. Carlos Santana, *Influences* DVD (Warner Brothers, 2003).

3. Nat Hentoff, liner notes to Gabor Szabo, *Spellbinder* CD (reissue, Impulse, 2005).

4. Darrin Fox, "Carlos Santana Spreads the Gospel of Tone," *Guitar Player*, May 2005, http://www.guitarplayer.com/article/carlos-santana-spreads/May-05/8870.

5. Shapiro, *Carlos Santana*, 136.

6. Deborah Santana, *Space Between the Stars: My Journey to an Open Heart* (New York: One World/Ballantine, 2006), 144.

7. Robert Christgau, "Consumer's Guide," Robert Christgau: Dean of Rock Critics, http://www.robertchristgau.com, and reprinted in his *Rock Albums of the 70s: A Critical Guide* (New York: Da Capo, 1990).

8. Santana, *Space Between the Stars*, 120.

9. Neil Leonard, "Carlos Santana: Musical Migration" *Rhythm Music Magazine* 3, no. 8 (August 1994), http://www.neilleonard.com/articles/santana.htm.

Rock guitarist Carlos Santana
performs for a crowd of an
estimated 1,000 inmates
in the recreation yard of
San Quentin prison on
December 10, 1988.
AP Photo/Jeff Reinking.

Carlos Santana performs his hit song "Maria, Maria," while taping The Tonight Show *with Jay Leno at NBC studios in Burbank, California, on February 24, 2000. Santana won eight Grammy awards at the annual presentation the night before. AP Photo/Reed Saxon.*

Carlos Santana accepts his award for pop/rock favorite band, duo, or group as Melissa Etheridge looks on at the American Music Awards on January 17, 2000, in Los Angeles. AP Photo/Kevork Djansezian.

Carlos Santana and his wife, Deborah, arrive at the Rock and Roll Hall of Fame induction ceremonies in New York on January 12, 1998. Santana, a group fueled by Carlos Santana's fiery guitar and dedication to Latin music and experimentation, was inducted to the Hall of Fame that year. AP Photo/Kathy Willens.

Guitarist Carlos Santana gestures during a news conference in Guatemala City on March 16, 2009. AP Photo/Moises Castillo.

Veteran rocker Carlos Santana sticks his tongue out at the crowd as he performs in Clarkston, Michigan, on June 12, 1999. AP Photo/Paul Warner.

Carlos Santana performs at Madison Square Garden on November 1, 1986. He joined other artists for this antidrug-themed concert. AP Photo/ Wilbur Funches.

Chapter 5

THE GUITARIST BRIDGING
CONTRADICTIONS

Carlos's musical path during the 1970s could be characterized as a series of swerves. He began the decade with a deep commitment to jazz rock—but in 1975 swerved away from the jazz-fusion style of *Caravanserai*, *Welcome*, and *Borboletta* and released *Amigos*, an album that was far more of a sales success than the jazz-fusion albums, and a recording that reflected the renewed presence of promoter and business manager Bill Graham in Carlos's career. Graham related a meeting he had with Carlos to *Rolling Stone* journalist Rich Wiseman. "'You had an ethnic, sweaty, street-star quality that everybody liked.... And you did something.... You continue to do it,' Graham said he told Carlos. 'You continue to do it, but in a more restrained way. You became refined. I don't like this refinement; you can make beautiful statements with your shirt off.'"[1]

This is Graham's version of their initial conversation before the recording of *Amigos*. Neither confirming nor denying Graham's story, Carlos told Wiseman about his musical change marked by *Amigos* in this fashion: "I'm still not looking at *Billboard*. But I do care about people. Touring with Earth, Wind & Fire made me realize that a lot of people are still waiting for the band Santana, not for any other reason than to receive what Santana, at one time, was offering them."[2] Carlos also informed Wiseman that he felt the music on *Amigos* was "sincere," and that sincere music has "life and joy." Whether the motive for *Amigos* was a recovery of "ethnic, street-wise, macho" identity as Graham depicted, or fan-pleasing as Carlos described, the recording began with advice from Graham that was difficult for Carlos to hear. Graham insisted upon having David Rubinson produce the album. Rubinson had been the producer at the first abortive attempt to record the original Santana band, a recording session marked by anger and disappointment felt by all. Rubinson and Carlos had no fond memories from that initial encounter. Yet Graham had faith that the pair could make amends and work together to create a new reincarnation of Latin rock with widespread commercial appeal. Rubinson had produced two significant Bay Area rock bands successfully, Jefferson Airplane and Moby Grape, and even produced a jazz pianist experimenting with pop in the 1970s, Herbie Hancock, a musician Carlos had long admired for his recordings with Miles Davis.

Sweetening Rubinson's re-entry was the enthusiasm Columbia Record executives felt about Santana's return to more commercial music signaled by Rubinson's production role. Wiseman notes that Columbia's pleasure with *Amigos* led to a new five-year, seven-album contract for Carlos with the most generous guarantees ever given to a rock musician at that time.[3]

Amigos also marked the return of bassist David Brown from the original Santana band and introduced the band's new drummer with was equally adept with rock and Latin rhythms, Ndugu Leon Chancler. The opening tune, "Dance Sister Dance (Baila Mi Hermana)," merges a New York salsa dance riff with Carlos's strong rock guitar solos. "Take Me with You" is an instrumental in two different moods. The first half is marked by fierce guitar soling by Carlos that makes the tune sound like an outtake from *Santana III*, the second a bit of a light jazz ballad. "Let Me" and "Tell Me Are You Tired" strongly change the Latin mood of most of the album by emphasizing funk, not unlike earlier recordings by Sly and the Family Stone and the funk-driven songs of Stevie Wonder.

Most remarkable is "Gitano," a composition in which Carlos seems to step aside from stage center and lets Armando Peraza, the band's veteran Afro-Cuban drummer, be in the spotlight. In a well-weathered, leathery vocal far removed from those smooth soul vocalists Carlos had mainly chosen in his career, Peraza sings what sounds like a leathery chant to the value of friendship in an extended Latin music jam filled with thrilling runs by keyboardist Tom Coster and spectacular drumming from Peraza. Carlos contributed his first acoustic guitar solo on record, one with strong flamenco touches. The aged and well-seasoned vocal presaged what older Cuban performers would do years later when they performed as the Buena Vista Social Club.

Another high point is a slowly seductive guitar showcase for Carlos, "Europa (Earth's Cry Heaven's Smile)." It quickly became one of the guitar-driven instrumentals most appreciated by fans. Its suave and gradually unfolding arrangement suggests an intricately composed love ballad. The gradual unfolding of "Europa" can be lucidly understood as an integral part both of Carlos's guitar style in particular and Latin music in general. As noted by Latino poet and essayist Victor Hernandez Cruz:

> Latin music, like Latin dance, follows a pattern; it starts out suave; the introduction, all the instruments do not come in at once; everything depends on the arrangement; the singer comes in and plants his theme, accompanied by a chorus which jumps in right after him, emphasizing the main poetic idea of the song; the orchestra grows toward an area where individual instruments can take a solo if it is in the calling; once this is over, they gather back on a plateau, which is similar to the intro; the music gathers momentum and rises to a take off area where they all accelerate together. This is the last area of frenzy and possession.[4]

Substitute "guitarist" for "singer" and "band" for "orchestra" and this is a cogent description of the structure of many Santana songs most immersed in Latin musical traditions. "Europa" is a highly romantic, even melodramatic composition, easily imaginable as a soundtrack for a film full of Latin American magic realism along the lines of *Like Water for Chocolate*. It conjures up Carlos's sensually dramatic solo on "Samba Pa Ti."

Festival, 1977's follow up to *Amigos*, bears a striking similarity on many levels to *Amigos*, though the presence of Armando Peraza is missed. Bassist David Brown was replaced by new band member Pablo Tellez. Percussionist Raul Rekow also became a valuable band member. And vocalist Greg Walker was replaced by—this is another example of the comings and goings of former Santana musicians—Leon Patillo, vocalist on *Borboletta*. Even with these changes, *Festival* has a striking similarity to *Amigos* in opening with a spirited Latin tune, then incorporating some funk songs, and having a guitar showcase for Carlos, "The River," that echoes in many regards the lyrical drama of "Europa."

But surpassing *Festival* that year in terms of both fan popularity and critical praise was *Moonflower*, a two-record set combining live and studio recordings, old and new band music. It was the first of several times in his career when Carlos would use the occasion of a new recording to cull an in-depth retrospective of Santana's history, an interest possibly created when *Santana's Greatest Hits*, a 1974 retrospective album compiled without any input from Carlos, offered severely edited versions of the band's early hits. *Moonflower* includes new versions of the earliest hits of the first Santana band, the show-stopper at the Woodstock Music Festival, "Soul Sacrifice," and the radio hit, "Black Magic Woman." It also offers more exuberant versions of studio material from *Amigos* and *Festival*. But the surprise hit of the album, and at first glance an unlikely hit, is the cover of a song by the Zombies, a UK band who had a U.S. hit with "She's Not There."

The original Zombies tune had catchy vocal harmonies, one brief solo on keyboards, a little electric guitar riffing, and energetic but basic 4/4 rock drumming. The Santana version reflects that special interaction that Carlos has always had with his keyboardists. Tom Coster opens the tune by repeating a simplified version of the melody on the marimba, with the first chiming notes ascending, the next phrase descending. This might have been the first rock song ever to open with a solo marimba, an instrument still rarely used out of classical and folk-music contexts. Coster's marimba repetitions are gradually joined by drumming and Carlos's guitar. Interestingly, Carlos doesn't take any solos until nearly halfway through the song. When he does, they are extremely dynamic, with quick flurries of high notes, and reintroducing the marimba melody with a baroque assortment of flourishes. A call-and-response between Carlos and the percussionists ensues. Then the song fades out as Carlos keeps propulsively soloing. The electric guitar's dominance, the interplay between Afro-Latin drumming and guitar, and the opening marimba feature—these cast the Zombies' original in a completely different light. In a sense, "She's Not There" can be interpreted as Carlos's response to Bill Graham's complaint that Carlos had grown too "refined" in his playing.

Rock 'n' roll from its origins in 1950s' America was conceived as a rebellion against middle-class, suburban values of "refinement. " The on-stage antics of the earliest rock stars broadcast that message loud and clear—Elvis Presley with his swaying pelvis, the absurdly silly duck walk guitar solos of Chuck Berry, and the mass media identification of early rock and roll with juvenile delinquency. An emphasis of extremely unrefined image and music came to a head in the mid-1970s with the birth of punk rock in the United Kingdom and the United States, and the birth of "hardcore" and various forms of "heavy metal" or "industrial" bands from the 1970s to the present. While those styles' extremes didn't appeal to Carlos, he did want in his own fashion to tune into his audience's expectations for unrefined musical abandon, and the guitar solos in *Moonflower* mark a step in that direction.

Moonflower is also remarkable because of the rounder and fuller guitar tone that Carlos achieves through experimentation with different guitar and amplifier combinations and a reconsideration of his fingerings on the guitar. Even on the live concert selections, which didn't capture the sonic clarity of the studio sessions, Carlos's playing sounds more grandly orchestral, yet also more mellow.

Carlos closed the seventies with yet another swerve, two albums that were enormously different from *Moonflower* and were, in fact, a genre unto themselves: spiritual program music. As the rest of Carlos's career would indicate, these two albums were exceptions to his overwhelmingly dominant, newfound commitment to mainstream pop music. There were certainly intimations of Carlos's desire to celebrate his spiritual guru, Sri Chinmoy, before, including putting his face on the cover photograph standing between Carlos and his musical collaborator, John McLaughlin. *Welcome* and the collaboration with Alice Coltrane, *Illuminations*, further emphasized Chinmoy's ideas. But *Oneness: Silver Dreams Golden Reality*, released in 1979, and *The Swing of Delight* were saturated with Chinmoy's personality, ranging from songs and poetry by Chinmoy to reproducing the guru's painting to serve as album cover art.

Oneness: Silver Dreams Golden Reality was truly a first in that it was a family affair for Carlos. His wife, Deborah, identified by the name given to her by Chinmoy, "Urmila," recites her guru's poetry, while Carlos's father-in-law, Saunders King, sings and plays rhythm guitar. Neither wholly rock nor jazz, the most dominant sound of the album is strings, both in the form of an actual string orchestra and synthesized strings. Carlos creates melodic solos against a near-constant wash of strings. An unusual cover of unlikely material for Carlos, the symphonic tone poem "Mysterious Mountain" by the contemporary composer Alan Hovhaness is perhaps the most memorable selection of the album. Hovhaness has been a composer with a long history of encoding feelings of mystical transcendence in his symphonies. That might explain why Carlos was attracted by the piece, which while crediting Hovhaness on the album, he renamed "Transformation Day." Sales of the album were slight in comparison to *Moonflower*, and while Carlos decided to keep on his musical and spiritual path, the accompanying musicians on *The Swing of Delight* might have represented a move to enhance marketplace acceptance.

Keyboardist Herbie Hancock, saxophonist Wayne Shorter, bassist Ron Carter, and drummer Tony Williams all had reputations in the jazz world as key members of the Miles Davis Quintet during the late 1960s. Each had quit Miles by the early seventies to pursue his own interests, with Hancock, Shorter, and Williams spearheading their own jazz-rock fusion bands. Carlos spoke of them as "the best musicians on the planet." And having them accompany Carlos on this project apart from his Santana band projects certainly added jazz credibility to his reputation. But *The Swing of Delight* was not seen as really either an authentic jazz or rock effort by many of Carlos's fans.

Over half of the original compositions created by Carlos were attributed by various listeners to variations on devotional songs by Chinmoy, particularly "Swapan Taari," "Phuler Matan," and "Jhama Kala." As the Indian titles suggest, these bore some resemble to Hindu devotional songs, mantras, meaning a repeated melodic evocation of key syllables to evoke divinity in a musical mode. They also had some resemblance to the compositions by John McLaughlin during his most intense time of devotion to Chinmoy when he led the Mahavishnu Orchestra, suggesting some raga-like riffs.

Two of the generally most successful tunes have no obvious tie to Chinmoy. Alex North's "Love Theme from 'Spartacus'" is a rousing film soundtrack anthem previously given jazz treatment by pianist Bill Evans and saxophonist Yusef Lateef. Whether or not Carlos had known their previous recordings, the tune's gradually unfolding melodrama probably caught his ear, not to mention the melody's attachment to a narrative of a freedom fighter and spiritual warrior, favorite archetypes for Carlos. The gentle interplay between Herbie Hancock on electric piano and Carlos is an example of highly thoughtful jazz improvisation on a memorable melody. Equally noteworthy is "Sher Khan," composed by Wayne Shorter, in which Carlos lets Shorter take stage center with a brooding, atmospheric soprano sax solo. The album's title foregrounding a key word in jazz, "swing," actually refers to "The Swing of Delight," a poem of Chinmoy's quoted on the album's back cover. The most intense moments of jazz swing spring from those moments when keyboardist Hancock and Carlos engage in instrumental cross-talk, continuing that often-noted special tie Carlos has always found with keyboardists.

These recordings did not lead Carlos deeper into his guru's circle. Exactly the opposite happened. In 1982 both Carlos and Deborah severed any connection with Chinmoy. Carlos told journalist Rick Ross that Chinmoy ranted against tennis champion Billie Jean King because of her lesbian identity and Carlos felt that dismissal was very unspiritual. The guru was so angry at Santana for leaving him, Santana told

Ross, that "he told all my friends not to call me ever again, because I was to drown in the dark sea of ignorance for leaving him."[5]

Busying himself in the 1980s in order to create a clean slate musically and spiritually, Carlos heavily impacted the Billboard charts with two of his most pop-sounding rock recordings, "Winning" from the album Zebop! and "Hold On" from Shango. "Winning" was originally written and performed by Russ Ballard and his group Argent, while "Hold On" was originally written and recorded by pop singer Ian Thomas. Both songs are classic rock anthems with no particular strong Latin music touches in their Santana interpretations. Both songs are nearly indistinguishable from songs performed by the band Journey, with ex–Santana members Gregg Rolie and Neal Schon.

While Zebop! was a commercial success, it was strongly criticized by many music critics for lacking unity. Nearly half of the album consists of instrumentals recalling the original Santana band ("Primera Invasion," "Tales of Kilimanjaro," "Hannibal," "American Gypsy," and a Jewish melody Bill Graham recalled from his youth, "I Love You Much Too Much"). The other half of the album consists of songs that both melodically and rhythmically sound like the product of any number of classic rock bands. The one exception is "E Papa Re," which contains a snippet of a few seconds of Afro-Cuban ritual chanting, an authentic ethnic touch surrounded by lyrics about some "natives" in a "jungle" dancing to some ritual around a fire. The nonspecificity of the lyrics play against the specific Afro-Cuban reference in the fleeting chant.

A similar type of uneasy reconciliation between typical pop rock and Latin roots occurred with the album following, Shango, although only three of its eleven tunes are instrumentals that recall the sound of the early Santana band. Two are particularly noteworthy. "Nueva York" marked the transitory return of original Santana keyboardist Gregg Rolie. The album's title track is essentially a percussive jam by the band's spirited percussion section, Raul Rekow, Orestes Vilato, and Armando Peraza. In terms of song lyrics, there was another cover of a Russ Ballard tune, "Nowhere to Run," and original songs by Carlos and other band members that purported to describe exotic African spiritual adventures ("The Nile" and "Oxun [Oshun])" which has the band's Scottish lead singer, Alexander Ligertwood, singing about when he was raised in a little African village in the heart of Kenya and being overcome by an evil spell that is eventually dissolved by a vision of the Virgin Mary. "Oxun (Oshun)" is the name of a West (not East African) African spirit transplanted through the Middle Passage of slavery to Latin America. It is known as Oxun or Oshun in Brazil in that country's Afro-Brazilian rituals currently. Whether Carlos simply was unaware of this, or took poetic license, is a matter of speculation. In any event, neither that particular song, nor the entire album, was seen as a highwater mark in Carlos's career.

Following these two albums, Carlos did *Havana Moon*, a solo project that enlisted a large variety of musicians he had never recorded with previously. These included keyboardist Booker T. Jones, the legendary leader of Booker T and the MGs, a major recording act performing Memphis soul music during the early 1960s, and the Texan rock guitarist Jimmie Vaughan and other members of his band, the Fabulous Thunderbirds. The Texas connection was implicit from the start of Carlos's career. Among the classic Texas blues guitarists who had strongly influenced Carlos's style were Lightnin' Hopkins, Clarence "Gatemouth" Brown, T-Bone Walker, and Freddie King. It was probably inevitable for Carlos to connect with the contemporaries bearers of the Texas blues tradition, the rocking blues guitarist Jimmie Vaughan, brother of Stevie Ray Vaughan, one of Carlos's long-time guitar idols. Another facet of that Texas connection that Carlos felt had to do with the fact that Texas popular music, like that of California, had long been flavored by Mexican influences.

The brass section of the Bay Area group Tower of Power, who worked on the *Santana III* album, returned to work with Carlos on this special project. Given the tensions that surrounded the first cooperative project with Tower of Power during the recording of *Santana III*, it must have a pleasure for Carlos as undisputed leader of his solo album to not have to argue for their participation. Country pop singer Willie Nelson also sang a tune and, most poignantly, so did Carlos's father José, closing the album.

Havana Moon was as close as Carlos would ever come to creating a largely chronological soundtrack of the influences that shaped him as a musician. He contributed cogent explanations about each tune, a useful guide for listeners who might otherwise have mistaken this as a randomly organized, "golden oldies" collection. The album opens with Bobby Parker's "Watch Your Step," which Carlos recalled hearing on the radio in Tijuana as a teenager. Parker's simple but hypnotic guitar riff unifying the song not only influenced Carlos's playing, but also turns up in slightly modified form on the Beatles' hit "Paperback Writer." While Parker rocked in R&B fashion, Lightnin' Hopkins, another early guitar influence on teenage Carlos, was more of a folk/blues–flavored Texas acoustic guitarist who performed original songs with unexpected twists and turns rhythmically and lyrically. Rather than rerecording a Hopkins song, Carlos created an instrumental, "Lightnin'," in which he joins Jimmy Vaughan and keyboardist Booker T. Jones in lightning-quick blues improvisation colored by the harmonica playing of Kim Wilson. Next is the Bo Diddley early rock classic, "Who Do You Love," which then segues seamlessly into a tribute to another great blues guitarist whose playing touched Carlos throughout his life, John Lee Hooker.

In an unusual move, Carlos included the instrumental "Tales of Kilimanjaro," which had recently been included on the *Zebop!* album, but in an earlier version that showcases an outstanding duet with keyboardist Alan Pasqua. The instrumental assumes an entirely new identity in the context of this musical autobiography, synthesizing Carlos's blues and Latin roots with clarity and grace. The album closes with two songs communicating wistfulness, longing, and romantically tinged memories. "They All Went to Mexico" is a kind of Mexicali blues that laments loved one who have all left the United States to return to Mexico. The words might have inspired Carlos in his first months as a teenager in the Bay Area desperately missing Mexico. It is a nostalgic ode to missing one's homeland. And the album closer, "Vereda Tropical," represents a complete musical and personal breakthrough for Carlos. It was a mariachi song that his father sang. Carlos wrote about the song in the liner notes:

> This is a song that I heard when I was a child. When my mom and dad had a lover's quarrel, we would wake up at 3 or 4 am to the sounds of music. . . . My mother would get up to peek through the curtains to see if the serenading was for her. She would always cry when she distinguished my father's voice singing to her.[6]

The courage and vulnerability Carlos demonstrated in narrating his musical (and by association, family history) on *Havana Moon* turned out to be a singular event. Implicit in bringing his father into the recording studio was a newfound acceptance of his faithful/faithless father, the father who nobly courted his mother into marriage, the man who repeatedly betrayed his marriage.

Carlos's next album, released in 1985, *Beyond Appearances*, was formulaic New Wave rock that plays down complex guitar solos by Carlos in favor of a sound dominated by two synthesizers and a drum machine. It was widely panned by both critics and fans, who found it difficult to discover much musical substance and original thinking "beyond appearances."

Distinguishing between Carlos's solo albums and the Santana band's albums had never been easy due to rapidly revolving rosters of musicians after the breakup of the original band of the first three albums. While one could claim the difference in labeling was useful—"Carlos Santana" was identified as the artist on the solo efforts like *Havana Moon* and *Santana* on a band album—the lines became blurry on a listening level after 1972. That distinction became as clear as it would ever be in 1987. *Freedom* was released by Santana and *Blues for Salvador* was released under the name Carlos Santana. It was a curious pair of releases for the same year. The Santana that recorded *Freedom* enlisted two veterans from Santana's early career, keyboardist Gregg Rolie and drummer/vocalist Buddy Miles. It also included Rolie's replacement, Tom Coster. But this group of veterans apparently was just passing through this incarnation of the Santana band since they would not record with Carlos again after 1987. Dominating *Freedom* is Buddy Miles, whose soulful vocals and powerhouse rock-funk drumming lead the session. In fact, a comparison of the previous collaborative recordings with Miles and Carlos reveals a highly restrained Carlos doing extremely clipped guitar solos complementing Miles. The earlier collaboration was a free-for-all of instrumental jamming with Miles's vocals taking more of a backseat. Synthesizers dominate the proceedings, as was the case with *Beyond Appearances*, though the two instrumentals, "Love Is You" and "Mandela," show that Carlos had not completely forgotten his roots in Latin music and jazz. Again, fans and critics largely ignored the album. Sales were very disappointing, though a world tour in support of the album brought renewed enthusiasm for Carlos throughout Europe and Asia.

In what might have seemed a tough move to reverse a musical slump, Carlos released one of the most musically powerful and sophisticated albums of his career, *Blues for Salvador*. Whatever distinctions can be made between his solo projects and Santana band projects, this album is a highwater mark, rapturously illuminating some of the finest guitar playing Carlos has ever recorded. Instead of reliance on the formulaic pop-rock riffs that marked his early 1980s music, *Blues for Salvador* is an original and impeccably sequenced set of instrumental revelations revealing the depth of Carlos's guitar style. While two tune titles pay homage to jazz masters who have deeply influenced Carlos, John Coltrane and Charles Mingus,[7] the deepest penetration into the heart of jazz guitar is the tune Carlos wrote for his daughter Bella. As Carlos explains on his music video *Influences*, "Bella" is both homage and summing up of the influence of the jazz guitarist Wes Montgomery upon him. Aptly, Carlos describes the "paternal tone" evoked by Montgomery's playing, making this composition from father Carlos to daughter Bella fitting. "Bella" is a lyrical flight with a gentle jazzy feel akin to some of the ballads Montgomery recorded toward the end of his life in the 1960s. A bit of that dreamy lyricism also characterizes the title tune, the "Salvador" referring to Carlos's son.

By way of complete contrast, "'Trane," which has a guest cameo by former Miles Davis drummer Tony Williams, gathers momentum like a steam locomotive going full bore. It is a bravura bit of rock-guitar improvisation, with keyboardist Chester Thompson and Latin drummer Armando Peraza egging Carlos on to daringly soar beyond his prior improvisations. Even more intense, dramatic, and uplifting is the live tune "Now That You Know" that teases at the edges of John McLaughlin's raga-flavored, India-centric, electric guitar-led fusion before moving into a guitar tapestry beyond category. It was culled from a live performance where audience shouts sound meaningful as Carlos ascends from one highly charged plateau to another dynamically in a loping solo that seems to mimic a runner leaping over Olympic hurdles. Not only was the album recognized as a milestone for Carlos, but he won a Grammy award for "Best Rock Instrumental" recording for it.

Much of the artistic triumph of Blues for Salvador was accomplished through a complex balancing act that Carlos had always bravely faced. He began as a blues player and then made the difficult transition to Latin rhythms in a synthesis with rock. By the time of Santana III, as his original successful band was coming apart at the seams, signs of a deep desire to make jazz improvisation part of the signature Santana band sound were emerging. Caravanserai, Welcome, Lotus, and Borboletta put the jazz connection front and center. The following albums seem to progressively diminish either the jazz or Latin elements, or both, and even seem to lessen the blues tines in Carlos's playing. Blues for Salvador literally sounds like it brings all of the previous musical styles back into a dynamic and entertaining, and ultimately surprising recombination.

The Grammy award and vigorous sales of Blues for Salvador might have smoothed over the periodically tumultuous relationship Carlos had with his recording company, but his creative restlessness got in the way of any lasting reconciliation with Columbia Records. The two projects following the album in the 1980s involved forming a jazz group with the famous jazz saxophonist Wayne Shorter, which included a popular concert at the Montreux Jazz Festival. That concert was recorded, but Columbia Records saw no sales potential for it and passed it up. This was surprising since Shorter was a key player in the jazz fusion band Weather Report, which was a commercial success for the company. In fact, Carlos played on the 1986 Weather Report album, *This Is This!* Nevertheless, the Santana-Shorter Montreaux band concert recording was not commercially available until 2005 as a CD and DVD on the Image label. It was a disappointment for Shorter also, who was drawing flack from jazz neoconservatives like Wynton Marsalis for ever agreeing to play with Carlos. But perhaps even more frustrating to Carlos and Columbia Records was the career retrospective of three discs that Carlos assembled in 1988, *Viva Santana.*

It has been common for pop musicians to tire of hearing and playing their hit recordings. And it has also been common for music companies, concerned about making profits, to want to compile discs consisting primarily or entirely of their most popular tunes. But by letting Carlos choose the program of his career retrospective, the greatest hits were often bypassed. Instead, half of the long box set (30 selections lasting nearly two and a half hours) consists of previously unreleased live and studio recordings, often of lesser-known Latin instrumentals. Columbia Records decided not to promote *Viva Santana* as vigorously as other Santana releases, leaving Carlos more interested in finding another music label than ever before. And that was exactly what he did in the 1990s, after fulfilling his contract with Columbia by creating one more original album.

In this musical overview of the 1980s, it should be noted that Carlos also spent much of that decade as a loving father to his three young children and as a generous donator of his time and talent on the concert stage for various charities and political causes he believed in. Among the charities he performed for: the Haight-Ashbury Medical Clinic, Farm Aid, and a range of services for underprivileged children. His political views could be characterized as broadly liberal, with support for unions, particularly United Farm Workers, led by Latino leader Cesar Chavez in the 1970s and 1980s, and for the rights of political prisoners, particularly those in South Africa where apartheid policies were raging during the 1980s. While other high-profile rock stars of the time also did charity concerts, many used the activity as an indirect way to self-advertise. Carlos did his charity work musically with a sense of quiet composure. In this way, his musical expression of "Love Devotion and Surrender" that characterized his involvement with spiritual guru Sri Chinmoy in the 1970s evolved into a public practice that continues today. Carlos learned to channel his desire for spiritual transcendence and oneness with the universe into practical acts of charity on a grand scale.

NOTES

1. Rich Wiseman, "Santana Comes Home: The Mission Street Mystic Returns to His Earthy Ways," *Rolling Stone*, May 6, 1976, http://www.rolling stone.com/news/story/5939974/cover_story_santana_comes_home.

2. Ibid.

3. Ibid.

4. Raul Fernandez, *Latin Jazz: The Perfect Combination* (San Francisco: Chronicle Books, 2002), 62.

5. Rick Ross, "Carlos Santana and Sri Chinmoy," February 29, 2000, www.rickross.com/reference/srichinmoy/srichinmoy18.html.

6. Liner notes to Carlos Santana, *Havana Moon* CD (Columbia CK 38642).

7. In his liner notes to the album, Carlos describes "Mingus" as "a mood" piece and indirectly makes a reference to a Mingus album entitled *Tijuana Moods*. Given Carlos's own musical experiences playing in Tijuana, it is understandable how the Mingus album spoke to him.

Chapter 6

MUSIC AND FAMILY
IN TRANSITION

The 1990s opened with Carlos ending his association with Columbia Records. This was the culmination of many years of frustration centered upon his perception that the company was not properly understanding and promoting his music. He needed to create one album in order to terminate his contract with Columbia Records in 1990, and that album was one of his most eclectic. Beginning with an original gospel choir composition, "Let There Be Light," *Spirits Dancing in the Flesh* includes covers of compositions by soul music master Curtis Mayfield, the Isley Brothers, and jazz giant John Coltrane as well as a revisit to a Santana band favorite from the first album, "Jin-Go-Lo-Ba" (originally titled "Jingo," an Afro-rock chant distilled from Olatunji's music).

As a parting offering to his recording company, it is a showcase of a full range of musical styles that Carlos convincingly and fervently performs. Unfortunately, from the company's point of view, it was another commercial failure, simply one of many post-1970s releases that weren't profitable. Carlos signed with Polydor Records, hoping for more rigorous promotion than was the case with Columbia Records.

At the same time, Carlos felt a need to develop musical connections with the younger generation of rock guitarists and bands, many of whom looked up to him as a "father figure" and mentor. Most significant in this regard was the bond Carlos formed with Trey Anastasio and the band Phish. A new generation's offshoot of the wildly improvisational spirit of the 1969 Santana band and the Grateful Dead, Phish was part of a style known from the 1980s on as "jam bands." Phish

opened for a number of Santana concerts in the 1990s, and the association seemed to add energy to everyone concerned.

The first album on the Arista label, *Milagro* (Spanish for "miracle"),
was very much the product of the feelings Carlos had for two friends
who recently died, Bill Graham and Miles Davis. Promoter and producer Bill Graham had been present through the decades, from the first
moment that Carlos had performed publicly on the stage at the Fillmore. Jazz trumpeter Miles Davis had opened for Carlos at the Fillmore
and shared his reverence for jazz in all of its various stylistic permuta-
tions. *Milagro* opens with a recording of Graham introducing Carlos
and the band as he had for so many years—and closes with a fragment
of a mournful yet determined Latin-tinged trumpet solo by Miles Davis
from his classic orchestral collaboration with composer Gil Evans,
Sketches of Spain.

Between these bookends was an album even more musically eclectic
than *Spirits Dancing in the Flesh.* In addition to incorporating Graham's
speaking voice and Davis's trumpet voice into the album, Carlos used a
moving bit of oratory, a portion of Dr. Martin Luther King Jr.'s "I've
Been to the Mountaintop" speech, as a preface to a deep gospel ballad
that compares King to Jesus, "Somewhere in Heaven." The juxtaposi-
tion of King and Jesus also underscores the integral connections Carlos
felt thrived among liberal politics, religious mysticism (particularly
Afro-Christianity), and music designed to encourage personal and societal liberation. This was a courageous set of ties for Carlos to champion
in 1992, given the drift toward extreme political conservatism initiated
by Ronald Reagan's presidency in the 1980s and continued by President George H. W. Bush into 1992. Religion and politics were linked
more closely during that conservative period—and the form of religion
linked to Reagan and Bush-style conservatism promoted sexual Puritan-
ism, the value of unfettered individualism and unregulated capitalism,
and a disinterest in the value of questioning the economic and political
status quo. Carlos identified strongly with the spiritual and political liberation of the 1960s as defined by the counterculture and in *Milagro*
was declaring that those 1960s values, the exact opposite of the era's
conservatism, were just as needed in the 1990s as decades ago.

Milagro also offers the first fruits of Carlos's interest in Jamaican reggae music. The album's title track appropriates the line "Free all the
people with music" from "Trench Town," a Bob Marley reggae anthem
released posthumously on Marley's *Confrontation* album. "Free All the
People (South Africa)" is entirely performed in reggae rhythm. "Agua
Que Va Caer" was the first all-out salsa jam that Carlos had recorded

since the title track to *Amigos*. And in a daring experiment, Carlos concludes the number with a taped excerpt of a powwow chant by the Bad River Singers, a Great Lakes Native people, perhaps to show the unity of all music of the Americas involved with changing listener consciousness, all music rhythmically thundered by those with the least political rights and economic prosperity.

And for the first time Carlos covered a song by a Motown star, "Right On," by Marvin Gaye. "Right On" was from *What's Goin' On*, the most overly political album Gaye ever made and the most musically eclectic. It was ideal for Carlos to cover, both in terms of the song's political content and due to the Latin-jazz feel of the song. "Right On" also reflects a type of Christian mysticism Carlos shared with Gaye, in which love would eventually triumph over the world's injustices. On Gaye's album, "Right On" segues into an original gospel tune, "Wholy Holy." That sudden tonal shift from the mainly political to chiefly religious that marked Gaye's *What's Goin' On* also strongly characterizes *Milagro*. The original gospel hymn "Somewhere in Heaven," cowritten by Carlos and his long-time vocalist Alex Ligertwood, has a middle section comprising a third of the nearly 10-minute recording in which Carlos plays a frenzied, full-speed-ahead, Latin-jazz instrumental, abruptly shifting from gospel hymn into a Latin jam session at full intensity, but then returning to the placid slow pace of the hymn. The song might be interpreted as a musical allegory about the oscillating need for acceptance (hymn) and rebellion (Latin jam) present in the souls of liberal religious and political reformers.

Although the album was no more profitable for his new label than his final album had been for Columbia Records, the guitar soloing that Carlos demonstrated on *Milagro* was particularly sharply etched. More than any previous Santana album, it was a bravura display of the full spectrum of musical styles Carlos had mastered by the 1990s. It also made explicit the specific mix of ancestral spirits to which Carlos constantly felt the need to pay homage. The sampled speech of Martin Luther King and the instrumental snippets from solos of saxophonists John Coltrane and Miles Davis that movingly close the album on the note of "A dios" surrounded Carlos and his listeners with the fire sources of his career. The cadences from King's speech were African, African American, and jazzy, simultaneously linking King to Davis and Coltrane, who also were strongly connected to the deep cultural roots in Africa and America to those cadences in the "I've Been to the Mountaintop" speech. Worth noting is that Carlos titled the close of *Milagro* "A dios," the unusual space in the Spanish word "Adios" revealing the original meaning of the phrase in medieval Spanish, "To be with God," " God's speed," or "May God be with you." The common modern understanding of "Adios" in America reduced the meaning to simply "goodbye." Carlos was emphasizing that Miles Davis and John Coltrane went to the house of God where they are still alive as sources of inspiration.

One result of the Santana band's 1993 world tour in support of the *Milagro* album was a series of particularly exciting concerts in Mexico City. The band on this tour was one in transition. Carlos's brother Jorge was added as a second, albeit restrained, guitarist. Myron Dove was a new bassist. Vocalist Vorriece Cooper supplemented vocalist Alex Ligertwood. For Carlos, playing with this new edition of the Santana band, which included his brother, very likely brought back memories of his family and cultural roots.

Two recordings culled from his Mexico City concerts were made. The CD of *Sacred Fire: Live in South America* consists of a 70-minute, 13-song mix of greatest hits from the past ("Soul Sacrifice," "Black Magic Woman," "Oye Como Va") and songs from *Milagro*. The film documentary entitled *Sacred Fire: Live in Mexico* includes five additional songs to the program and lasts an hour and a half. Curiously, several of the most exciting tunes, with stellar guitar solos played by Carlos, including a super-charged version of "Spirits Dancing in the Flesh" and "Batuka," were left off the CD. Part of the power of the documentary film, in contrast to the CD, also involves seeing Carlos walking with his guitar through his homeland. An additional plus to the documentary film is seeing the ecstatic reception the Mexican fans give to one of their own. While the CD sales were even more disappointing than *Milagro*, the film on video and DVD has sold well internationally. It has been well received during the several occasions it was offered on public television in the United States.

REUNITING WITH HIS FAMILY MUSICALLY

Although Jorge, Carlos's younger brother, was not heard from to any great extent on the Mexican City concerts, that changed radically with the 1994 release of *Santana Brothers*. Carlos teamed up with Jorge, who had written a great deal of original material since disconnecting with his band Malo and being removed from any active music scene. Joining them to complete a family guitar trinity was Carlos's nephew, Carlos Hernandez. The backup band supporting the guitarists was largely comprised of the same musicians who performed on the international tour in support of *Milagro*.

Several elements distinguish *The Santana Brothers* from any of the previous 28 albums appearing under the Santana name. It is entirely an instrumental showcase for electric and acoustic guitar virtuosity. The opening selection, "Transmutation/Industrial," is an unusual mix of ambient and heavy metal rock, another first for Carlos, and a nod in some fashion to jazz/heavy metal rock guitarist Sonny Sharrock, who died in 1994, the year the album was released.[1] The tune also makes explicit the friendship Carlos had recently developed with Vernon Reid, guitarist and leader of the heavy metal rock–jazz–funk band Living Color. Reid had produced some tracks for *Spirits Dancing in the Flesh*. And in yet another bow to a musical ancestor, Carlos took the theme that jazz trumpeter Miles Davis improvised upon on his *Sketches of Spain* album, a classical melody by the Spanish composer Joaquin Rodrigo, and set it to a reggae rhythm. Of the album's eleven instruments, one is a solo effort by Carlos, "Blues Latino," a piece in the lyrical spirit of "Samba Pa Ti," one is a pastoral acoustic guitar piece by Jorge, "Mornings in Marin," and one is a Latin rocker by Carlos Hernandez. The remaining tunes are family jams. The family theme is also underscored by the photo collage Carlos chose for the album cover. Before portraits of himself, his brother, and nephew, Carlos positioned two large cradling hands. A tinted photograph of his father as a young man in his mariachi band days is joined with a photograph of his father-in-law, R&B guitarist Saunders King, marking the album as honoring the musical ancestors within the family circle.

Unfortunately from Polydor's standpoint, this family affair was less than a commercial success, not equaling in sales the first two albums Carlos did for the label, so Carlos sensed that the time might be ripe to go shopping for yet another musical company. He also found himself well in middle age and far removed from chart-topping rap groups, a formidable 1960s icon of innovative rock guitar without a relevant contemporary context through the 1980s and 1990s. A major influence on hit-making Latin rock bands of Los Lobos and Ozomatli in the 1990s, Carlos found himself disconnected from their massive audiences.

A CAREER RETROSPECTIVE FROM HIS FORMER RECORDING LABEL

Career retrospectives of the recordings of popular musicians have often been haphazard music company assemblages that have little connection to what the musician might have wished to be included. Such a collection was the one released by Columbia Record in the 1970s under the title of *Santana's Greatest Hits*, a seemingly random sample from the first three Santana band albums. In 1988, when Columbia Records proposed a more capacious selection from their back catalogue, Carlos presented a plan for three albums containing the less commercially appealing band tunes from the past two decades, or "hits" in previously unreleased concert versions. The result was the compilation *Viva Santana*, which settled for a middle ground between the recording company's wishes and the artist's.

The 1995 compilation, *Dance of the Rainbow Serpent*, features an explanatory booklet penned by Carlos that offers highly detailed and personalized interpretations and memories attached to his songs. The compilation's three-disc organization used categories suggested with Carlos's direct input: "Heart," "Soul," and "Spirit." Carlos also offers an engagingly original interpretation of the compilation's title in his preface:

> What is the dance of the rainbow serpent? I think of it like this: the blood that flows through our veins makes it possible for us to have balance and coordination like the minerals that flow through the earth. Without that blood dancing through our bodies man is not whole. Without minerals dancing through our mother earth there can be no balance. The dance of blood and minerals is what keeps the balance on the planet. . . . This collection of music is my dance.[2]

The symbol of the rainbow serpent was not a uniquely imaginative invention by Carlos. It has been a key symbol in the mythology of Australian Aboriginals for centuries. It has portrayed for them both the creation and destructive powers of the earth. There has been even a ritual dance to portray the rainbow serpent moving to music.[3] As has been the case with influential jazz and blues musicians, Carlos has always felt free to develop his own spiritual style through creatively blending eclectic learning. In response to interviewer Steve Heilig's question, "I'm wondering if you have a 'label' for your faith, your spirituality, like Christian, Buddhist, etc. . . . " Carlos replied: "Well, hopefully, it's like water, you know; water is very powerful, but very humble. . . . To spread the message of kindness to everybody . . . kindness and redemption—a win-win situation for people and the planet—that's my religion."[4]

This spiritual borrowing from many different religious traditions stood in marked contrast to the days when Carlos defined his spirituality solely within the dictates of the belief of Sri Chinmoy. And while members of the press were often disconcerted with hearing Carlos explain his music through a rainbow serpent or an angel, few doubted his sincerity and willingness to translate his spiritual beliefs into global acts of charity.

AN ACT OF CHARITY BEFORE INCUBATING THE "SUPERNATURAL"

Carlos characteristically looked inward during those five years after the release of *The Santana Brothers*, doing a great deal of soul searching spiritually as well as musically. The first public action suggesting that Carlos might be dramatically rethinking his career and purpose was the founding of the Milagro Foundation with his wife Deborah in 1998. While major rock musicians turning over part of their income to charity has been a regular activity of many stars over the years, the Milagro was a financially vibrant, sustained, well-organized, and sharply focused charity effort dedicated to alleviating the suffering of children in poverty through offering educational and counseling opportunities. By institutionalizing his interest in the needs of underprivileged children, Carlos connected to memories of his own harsh youth—but also did something more. He directed his musical focus to the challenge of creating original music that could speak across generational gaps by meeting universal human needs.

The origin of rock music was mired in the youth culture of the 1950s. From Chuck Berry to Elvis, teenagers could identify with music their parents despised. This generation gap was widened during the sixties as rock became identified with experimental sexual activity and drug use, two more-horrifying-than-ever activities to parents. Recording companies have traditionally targeted much rock music to a 15- to 25-year-old demographic; not only is this group most identified with a rebellious music style, but it is also the group that possesses the most disposable income. In fact, mass exposure for Carlos and the Santana band came through the recording and later documentary film of the Woodstock Music Festival that literally put rock music on Wall Street through marketing youthful rebellion as a profitable commodity.

Carlos had learned through his association with manager Bill Graham to try to balance his musical idealism with the need to maintain status as a profitable musician. The meaning of "profitable" had undergone radical change since Carlos had entered the music business.

The 1960s was the first decade where popular rock musicians were commonly millionaires and had lifestyles that needed millions to support. Carlos was exceptional in being a millionaire star without needing millions to support an ostentatious, materialistic lifestyle. Beyond giving millions to charity, one wondered what kept Carlos wanting to make millions more? Was it a type of "famine mentality" common to immigrants who had suffered poverty in their homeland and never wanted to risk sinking back into poverty? Curiously, several astrologers have posted on the Internet their assessment of Carlos's personality based on his horoscope. One reads:

> Carlos SANTANA, the nocturnal North-eastern quadrant, consisting of the 1st, 2nd and 3rd houses, prevails in your chart: this sector favours self-assertion and material security to the detriment of your perception of others. You consider self-transformation to be a hazardous adventure. You are inclined to seek stability and you tend to protect yourself with your actions. Possession, acquisition but also communication, without opening up too much, are part of your deep motivations. You are rather autonomous and constant, however it is important that you pay more attention to others, so that you can improve your outcomes.[5]

Perhaps a more direct influence upon Carlos's view of financial security than the stars was Bill Graham, who shared with Carlos a severely traumatic childhood and learned to amass millions of dollars in a never-ending quest for financial security.

When Graham died in a helicopter crash in 1992, Carlos lost a friend and music-business mentor. That need for a kind of "father figure" in the music business did not disappear after Graham's death. Fortunately, Carlos found such a figure in Clive Davis, a singular record executive who founded Arista Records in the 1970s after being fired by Columbia Records. Like Graham, Davis hailed from a working-class Jewish background and had a "rags to riches" story as dramatic as Graham's in its own way.

Arista Records, prior to signing Carlos, had both a rock-pop identity and an avant-garde jazz identity, a bold venture where the rock profits were recycled into sustaining the "Arista Freedom" label that released major music by the adventurous Ornette Coleman, Albert Ayler, Anthony Braxton, and saxophonist and former Coltrane colleague Archie Shepp. Carlos had admired Shepp a long time, so the fact that

Davis was promoting his music undoubtedly boded well. Another vote of confidence for Davis as a jazz adventurer was that he released music performed by trumpeter Don Cherry, a friend of Carlos as well as the father of a musician Carlos would soon be in the recording studio with, Eagle-Eye Cherry. Finally, Davis released an album showcasing Argentinean tenor saxophonist Gato Barbieri doing duets with the exiled South African pianist Dollar Brand. Barbieri, who shared Carlos's adoration for John Coltrane's music, came to appreciate Carlos and his music. Barbieri in the 1970s recorded in a moody bolero version, clothed in strings, of a composition by Tom Coster and Carlos, "Europa (Earth's Cry Heaven's Smile)." Carlos joined Barbieri in the recording studio for "Latin Lady," which appeared on a Barbieri album entitled *Tropico*.

Another facet of Clive Davis that Carlos found attractive was his commitment to rejuvenate the careers of singers and bands who had fallen into hard times since their glory days in the 1960s. The two outstanding examples were Aretha Franklin, always admired by Carlos, and closer to his musical homeground, the Grateful Dead. Interestingly, Davis was immortalized in a Grateful Dead revision of their song "Jack Straw" as the one whose friendship they played for, a tribute echoing the gratitude the band Aerosmith expressed toward Davis in their song "No Surprise."

In a filmed interview about his signing Carlos to Arista Records Davis commented that he found Carlos "hungry" for getting radio play again in the 1990s.[6] Davis knew that Carlos, "hungry" as he was for recharged stardom, was not about to simply buy into a new concept. So Davis listened patiently while Carlos told Davis about talking with spirits. Santana claimed to have been contacted by the Virgin of Guadalupe while praying. He also has told interviewers about an angel contact in the mid-1990s. "You will be inside the radio frequency for the purpose of connecting the molecules with the light," the angel told him. "Be patient, gracious and grateful."[7]

While Carlos was maintaining a heavenly vision, Davis was thinking about cross-generational connections that would help Carlos craft a hit album. Davis thought back to the sixties when he met with English rock guitar master Eric Clapton—and forward into the nineties when he spoke with Lauryn Hill, Everlast, Rob Thomas of Matchbox Twenty, and Eagle-Eye Cherry. Davis presented to Carlos an album concept in which musical "friends" across generations would record with Carlos in order to portray a spiritual and musical odyssey of one soul through a mélange of Afro-Cuban rhythms.

The resulting album, *Supernatural*, became the most massively popular album of Carlos Santana's career and won eight Grammy awards.

How many of the 25 million worldwide who purchased *Supernatural* were aware of a unifying theme linking the 11 tunes is unknowable. Millions came to discover the album primarily through radio-friendly hits that included "Smooth," a rocker with a cha-cha rhythmic undertow sung by Rob Thomas, and the ballad "Love of My Life" cowritten by Carlos with Dave Matthews shortly after Carlos's father's death. Carlos had been haunted by a classical melody he could not identify and went to a Tower Records store in California and sang the melody to a sales assistant very knowledgeable in classical music. The clerk led Carlos to a recording of Brahms' Piano Concerto no. 2. Then Carlos mined the bittersweet melody as he was coping with his lachrymose feelings associated with his father's death. And Dave Matthews crafted the right tone for the ballad filled with longing.

Another song full of emotional intensity was "Put Your Lights On" by Everlast (aka Erik Schrody), a gruff-voiced rapper and singer-songwriter who wrote the song as he was coming out of a life-threatening illness. The guitar solo supporting Everlast carries an appropriate urgency for one who has made such a difficult passage. On a lighter note, "Maria Maria" is a simple song with a strong Latin flavor because of strong acoustic guitar trills from Carlos, a lyrical wink to the first Latin-themed Broadway musical, *West Side Story*, and lyrics modulating between Spanish and English.

Officially ending the album with a guitar duet in a mid-tempo shuffle is British rock star Eric Clapton. Clapton was a reminder for long-time Santana fans (who remembered his ascent in 1969) that Carlos was still connecting with the best musicians in rock who had prospered as times changed. But Carlos also "unofficially" ends the album with a powerhouse instrumental that is nowhere credited on the album's liner notes, "Victory Is Won." It is not the full version, which was later released on the *Supernatural Live Santana* DVD and then as part of Carlos's next album, *Shaman*. The unidentified version that begins where the Clapton collaboration ends is a dramatically ascending blend of rock anthem and Spanish bolero with a memorable melody that Carlos begins to fragment into shards of dissonant runs exactly as the recording fades and the album ends. This "mystery cut" might have served as a warning to critics (whom Carlos suspected would accuse him of commercially "selling out") that the unconventional and jazzy player who loved Coltrane and Sonny Sharrock is still alive and well.

Supernatural sold over 25 million albums internationally and brought Carlos eight Grammy awards at the 42nd Annual Grammy Awards held February 23, 2000. For one musician to win that many Grammys in one ceremony had occurred only once before—Michael Jackson for *Thriller* in 1983. In recognition of his support, Carlos pulled producer Clive Davis up on stage to share the applause. The Grammy awards included "Song of the Year" for "Smooth" and "Album of the Year" for *Supernatural*. In his acceptance speech, Carlos spoke about the relation of his music to spirituality while thanking his family, fellow musicians, and recording company colleagues. Not only was that evening an affirmation of Carlos's career, it was also the beginning of widespread public awareness that Latin music was now "mainstream" American music.

Ironically that same year, the organization sponsoring the Grammy awards, the National Academy of Recording Arts and Sciences, created a separate award ceremony for Latin music because a number of Hispanic musicians, most visibly Latin pop star Gloria Estefan, felt too marginalized within the context of the regular Grammy award process. So the Latin Grammy Awards were held seven months after the general Grammy award ceremony. And again, with a sense of déjà vu surrounding the proceedings. Carlos proved to be overpoweringly successful in winning three Grammys.

Yet the commercial success of *Supernatural* also left Carlos vulnerable when he went on tour to support the album. This point was made by Tom Sinclair, a music journalist for *Entertainment Weekly*:

> It's no secret Santana's *Supernatural* owes its success partly to his high-profile guests. But when he kicks off a U.S. tour July 20, will kids be bummed to find hired guns Tony Lindsay and Andy Vargas singing the hits—not Rob Thomas ("Smooth") or the Product G&B ("Maria Maria")? "People want to hear the songs sounding somewhat like they do on the radio, and Carlos definitely delivers," says Santana rep Susan Stewart. She adds that Everlast will join the tour's second leg and will "most likely" perform "Turn Your Lights On." Uh, we'll most likely stick with the CD.[8]

The "Carlos with Friends" approach developed by Clive Davis could work to perfection only within a recording studio environment where scheduling and overdubs could be easily arranged. When Carlos burst upon the music scene in 1969 he was the guitarist of a cohesive band that toured nonstop internationally, an ensemble always capable of recapturing its recorded sound live. That transfer of recorded music to concert stage differentiated rock music sharply from jazz, where fans attended concerts with the desire not to hear a recorded version of a tune, but a very different, improvised version. But Carlos put aside the concern about pleasing crowds with note-for-note replications of *Supernatural* and continued to seek out Davis's business advice.

Another vulnerability opened by *Supernatural* was the dilution of the Latin music keystone of Carlos's sound. Latin percussion was pushed to the background as young vocalists assumed center stage with Carlos. This created the possibility of losing a Baby Boomer audience who associated Carlos completely with the interplay instrumentally of guitar and Latin percussion. One sign of this disconnect was the film released on DVD of a concert at the Pasadena Civic Auditorium in support of the album.[9] The concert opens with "(Da Le) Yaleo," a Latin-flavored dance number that includes less than a minute of Carlos exchanging licks in a call-and-response with conga player Raul Rekow and timbales player Karl Perazzo. The dominant solos are supplied solely by Carlos and keyboardist Chester Thompson, and the dominant image filling a video monitor are dancing girls in sexy Brazilian carnival, feather-festooned attire who are filmed at angles that block a clear view of Rekow and Perazzo. Even the film's opening credits make a point of listing the star vocalists before citing instrumentalists, let alone percussionists. From a commercial point of view, this made the filmed concert of *Supernatural* more of an event reaching across all audience demographics, the dream of pop-music marketers. From a musical point of view, the documentary downplayed the specifically Latin ethnic flavors that endeared Carlos to a Latino and white countercultural audience (who wished they were Latino).

WHAT CAREER DIRECTION AFTER *SUPERNATURAL*?

Carlos once again looked to Clive Davis for a sense of musical direction as well as financial advice after the overwhelming commercial success of *Supernatural*. Davis and Carlos agreed to repeat the same formula as *Supernatural*: a "Carlos Santana with his young vocal friends" format. There were two musical deviations, however. For *Shaman*, the ethereal-sounding title of the album, Carlos would not rely upon rock performers on the order of Eric Clapton and Dave Matthews. Instead, there would be a greater emphasis on pop, exemplified by the 19-year-old vocalist Michelle Branch who had scored a hit single with "The Game of Love." The terse guitar solo complimenting Branch made Carlos seem like a servant to her tune in the opinion of many music critics and fans of the older, more Latin-tinged Santana albums.

Perhaps the most enjoyable facet of Carlos's solo on Branch's hit were his flurry of heart-fluttering notes, simpatico with the lyrics. As on a number of other *Shaman* tunes, it is difficult to hear the usual interplay between Carlos's guitar and conga drums, the hand drums on this song overwhelmed in the sound mix by drum machines.

A more striking change from *Supernatural* would be the first recordings Carlos ever made of pop music from the African nation of Benin, "Adouma," as composed by the Afro-Parisian diva Angelique Kidjo. The bouncy, polyrhythmic tour de force that energetically opened *Shaman* was arguably an advance for Carlos, incorporating successfully the African roots of his American music. Another new direction for Carlos was the song "Foo Foo" by the dynamic Haitian pop band Tabou Combo, who performed in a musical style known as Compas, a highly danceable mix of various Latin dance styles including merengue and mambo, and perhaps even having rhythmic roots in Haitian voodoo. Carlos demonstrated on "Foo Foo" a remarkable fluency with the style.

The rap numbers on *Shaman* appeared to many listeners as less successful than those on *Supernatural*. The song "Since Supernatural" featured the lyrics, "Since 'Supernatural' ain't nothin' much happened," which could be misunderstood as an assessment of creative doldrums in Carlos's career in the post-*Supernatural* period. And in what might have been a first and last, opera tenor Placido Domingo, no stranger to popmusic collaborations, sang a melody partially written by an early guitar idol of Carlos's, Gabor Szabo, backed by Carlos and a thick blanket of string players. Although Carlos had wrapped his guitar solos with layers of strings on his collaboration with Alice Coltrane, the string arrangement of *Shaman* conjured Hollywood film soundtrack music rather than ethereal New Age musical journey.

A far more appropriate match was with the band Ozomatli, a Latin–funk–hip-hop band who were inspired by the earlier decades of Carlos's career. Ozomatli, along with Los Lonely Boys, has carried the Latin rock charge into the 21st century. "One of These Days" makes one wonder what the album might have been as an adventure if Carlos had recorded entirely with the young Latin musical revisionists.

Given this grab-bag expansion, though not necessarily refinement, of the "Carlos and friends" formula that worked so well on *Supernatural*, sales of *Shaman* were rigorous, but not as overwhelming as that of its predecessor. Yet this did not stop Clive Davis and Carlos from trying the "supernatural" formula one more time in 2005. But before that third installment of "Carlos Santana and Friends" came a major, one-off milestone in Carlos's career.

LIVE AT MONTREUX JAZZ FESTIVAL 2004: FOR PEACE, FOR HEALING MUSIC

The Montreux Jazz Festival, a highly prestigious music event that has drawn musicians internationally since 1962, was the brainchild of Claude Nobs, who became the festival's director. Carlos and Nobs established a friendship in 1970, and one consequence was the appearance of the Carlos Santana–Wayne Shorter Band at the 1988 Montreux Festival. Connecting Carlos, Shorter, and Nobs was their deep friendship and sense of musical affinity with the great jazz trumpeter Miles Davis. Although Davis was seriously ill and limited concert performances in the late 1980s, Carlos held on to a dream of a super-concert at Montreux with Davis and many of the musicians associated with him.

But Davis died the same year he made his final concert appearance at Montreux, 1991, though he was survived by many of his musical colleagues. Twelve years later, when Nobs asked Carlos what he wanted to present at Montreux, Carlos realized a gathering of former Miles Davis colleagues along with the New Santana Band and some special guest vocalists would be a highly worthwhile occasion. But because Carlos had never separated his musical from his spiritual and political idealism, he wanted the concert's musical program to be entitled "Hymns for Peace." As Carlos explained in his notes to the DVD of the event:

> Today is the beginning of tomorrow. I truly believe that these new songs were assigned and designed by their authors, Bob Dylan, Bob Marley, John Lennon, Marvin Gaye, and John Coltrane, to give birth to a new consciousness. . . . In the past, certain religious songs were made for Hebrews, Muslims, Buddhists, or Christians only. However, these spiritual songs bring healing and illumination to all humanity.[10]

Carlos spent much of the year leading up to the 2004 Montreux Jazz Festival arranging for Miles Davis's former musical colleagues to join for this ambitious undertaking. The result, which was edited into a three-hour film, reveals Carlos performing at the top of his game, music radically different for the most part in style and substance from that on the *Supernatural* and *Shaman*. The largest difference can be summed up by the word *improvisation*. Carlos relished the opportunity to stretch out musical ideas with jazz veterans of the caliber of keyboardists Herbie Hancock and Chick Corea, saxophonist Wayne Shorter, and guitarist John McLaughlin. There was also a powerful cross-generational element inspiring the musicians by the inclusion of John Coltrane's son, saxophonist Ravi Coltrane, and by Carlos's son Salvador, who performed lyrically on keyboards. One of the highlights of the event is a sensitive duet between the two on a jazz tune identified with John Coltrane's colleague, saxophonist Pharoah Sanders, "Light at the Edge of the World."

Of the 26 tunes performed during the *Hymns for Peace*, only two had been previously recorded by Carlos, "Adouma" and "Jingo," and these were performed at Montreux with far more improvisation off their African polyrhythms than on their original recordings. John Coltrane's music was celebrated through a spirited version of one of his most Latin-flavored recordings, "AfroBlue," an excerpt from "Peace on Earth" and a rendition of a major theme from Coltrane's *A Love Supreme*. While some of the rock and pop songs drew less than inspired performances from the musicians, the obvious enthusiasm that Carlos demonstrated throughout the concert seemed to move the audience and critics alike. Carlos was clearly the "glue" that held the concert together, and while only Carlos would program Coltrane's pensive "Peace on Earth" to segue into John Lee Hooker's "Boogie Woman," a jarring transition for any musician to bridge tastefully, there is no question that the jazz musicians seemed to enjoy themselves thoroughly in realizing this ambitious concert blending rock and jazz.

Another measure of Carlos's success was revealed in a filmed interview after the concert where he remarks that "there are certain events—Woodstock, The Concert for Amnesty International—where the whole world beholds the goodness in every person."[11] The mutual admiration and respect evidenced by the concert film support that perception and give credence to the sense that his music is, in a term Carlos favors in describing his music, "healing."

Yet another landmark for Carlos at Montreux 2004 was his role was largely the producer of a blues program presenting three older bluesmen who had long been guitar inspirations for him: Bobby Parker, Clarence "Gatemouth" Brown, and Buddy Guy. While Carlos occasionally let himself take leading solos, his role was largely supportive, a selfless honorific gesture, particularly to the 80-year-old and seriously ailing Brown, whose career had never achieved the commercial success that Carlos had long known. A year after his Montreux concert, Brown lost his home to the effects of Hurricane Katrina and then died from lung cancer. By assuming the mantle of a concert producer for often-undervalued blues musicians, Carlos had come full circle and reconnected with his own youth as an unknown blues guitar asking concert producer Bill Graham for a chance to perform. Always concerned with delineating the lines of musical history, Carlos underscores in his liner notes to the DVD set of this event, "All of these musicians paved the road for Eric Clapton, Michael Bloomfield, Peter Green, Jeff Beck, Jimmy Page and me."[12]

ALL THAT CARLOS IS?

A year following these pan-stylistic triumphs at Montreux was the release of the album *All That I Am*, a claim many long-time Santana fans and critics disagree with. The guitar solos, with the exception of "Trinity," are more concise and ancillary to the vocalists than ever before, making Carlos more than ever sound like a mere accompanist to a potpourri of stars. And with the exception of the opening two tunes, the rousing "Hermes" and "El Fuego," which are charged with African and Caribbean rhythms, the remainder of the album is middle-of-the road rock-pop music, music tailored to radio-formatting. Perhaps "Trinity," a three-way rock instrumental, conjuring up memories of *The Santana Brothers* CD, is most successful in showcasing how Santana's soloing can be as piquant and creative as ever. But unlike the interplay with his brother Jorge and his nephew, heavy-metal Metallica guitarist Kirk Hammett and pedal steel guitarist Robert Randolph did not venture into open-ended styles like jazz or ambient, so Carlos was not presented with as much opportunity to exercise his genre-crossing creativity. Of the rap numbers, the uplifting moral message of "I Am Somebody" showcasing rapper will.i.am, seems to capture something of Carlos's idealism and stands out from the rest of the rap material. In spite of these shortcomings, sales were fairly robust since music from the album was intensely appropriated for advertisements for one of the 21st century's most popular entertainment technologies, the iPod Nano, manufactured by Apple Computers.

By 2005, Carlos had licensed products using his name to a line of women's stylish shoes, hats, men's apparel and neckware, percussion, candles, body lotions, sunglasses, and inspirational cards and journals. Some of the proceeds from these items, as well as from his music, went directly into the nonprofit Milagro Foundation for underprivileged children. Carlos also generously gave free public concerts often for worthy causes, like AIDS education in Africa, a cause for which he gave 100 percent of his concert profits to during a 23-city tour in 2003.[13] Carlos was now a super-wealthy pop star, the culmination of a classic American "rags to riches" story. He had disproved the belief of the writer F. Scott Fitzgerald that American successes stories never had "a second act."

Yet the year 2007 would throw a disruptive twist into this "rags to riches" story.

NOTES

1. This album is dedicated to Sonny Sharrock, along with other guitarists associated with rock and blues as well as jazz: Albert Collins, Eric Gale, Joe Pass, and Craig Lasher.

2. Booklet accompanying Santana, *Dance of the Rainbow Serpent* (Columbia Legacy C3K64605).

3. See the online edition of the *Coffs Coast Advocate* for additional information about the Australian aboriginal meaning of the rainbow serpent's dance, http://www.finda.com.au/story/2008/09/24/welcome-return-for-the-rainbow-serpent/

4. Steve Heilig, "The World of Carlos Santana," *The Beat* 19, no. 1 (2000): 73.

5. "Carlos Santana: Astrology and Birth Chart," http://www.astrotheme.com/portraits/53SpZq3R25by.htm.

6. Carlos Santana, *Supernatural Live* DVD.

7. "Supernatural by Santana and Friends," http://www.sfmission.com/santana/supernatural.htm.

8. Tom Sinclair, "Tours de Force," *Entertainment Weekly*, June 23, 2000, http://www.ew.com/ew/article/0,85306,00.html (accessed February 24, 2009).

9. *Supernatural Live Santana*, DVD (Arista 07822-15750-9, 2000).

10. Santana: *Hymns for Peace: Live at Montreux 2004*, DVD (Eagle Eye Media EE 39144-9).

11. "Carlos Santana: Astrology and Birth Chart."

12. *Carlos Santana Presents Blues at Montreux*, DVD (Eagle Eye Media EE 39127-9).

13. "Rock Musician Carlos Santana Raises $2 Million for South African AIDS Group on 23-City Concert Tour," July 16, 2003, retrieved from The Body: The Complete HIV and AIDS Resource, http://www.thebody.com/content/art/art6774.html.

Chapter 7

LEAVING MARRIAGE, SPARKING CONTROVERSY, REINVENTING HIS STYLE

An Associated Press story filled with speculation ran on November 2, 2007, under the banner headline of "Carlos Santana, Wife Getting Divorce." Only two undisputable facts were in the story. One was that Deborah Santana filed for divorce in the Marin County, California, Superior Court on the grounds of irreconcilable differences. The other was that Michael Jensen, Carlos's personal publicist, described the case as "a private matter and there is no comment."[1] The tabloid speculation of the cause was Carlos's sexual infidelity, a transgression he publicly acknowledged after Deborah wrote about it in her memoir, *Space Between the Stars*.

Whether Carlos or Deborah ever decides to disclose his or her individual interpretation of the divorce, the very fact that a popular celebrity musician's divorce made a wire service statement as news was a tribute to the rare longevity and publicly displayed devotion of their marriage. In the United States, where half of all marriages end in divorce, and the divorce rate of celebrities has always seemed to wildly exceed that statistic, it was remarkable that this marriage endured as it had. It was also worth noting that this divorce was not filed until two of their three children were out in the world on their own, and the third was on the threshold of doing so.

How sudden the decision was on Deborah's part was hard to discern. Earlier that year, they had appeared harmoniously in public to announce their intention to start a Mexican restaurant named "Maria." The restaurant name, they said, was inspired by the song of the same name on

Supernatural. Ironically, those lyrics compared the Maria of the song to the Maria of the Broadway musical *West Side Story*, a lover whose love led ultimately to her tragic demise, though one would have been hard put earlier in 2007 to cast the 34-year marriage in such a tragic light.

On the contrary, when Carlos prepared in 2007 *Multi-Dimensional Warrior*, his two-CD retrospective set of personally chosen instrumentals and songs from the past three decades, he penned the following words to Deborah for the CD booklet: "Deborah—for your impeccable integrity, gentle wisdom, and soulful spirit.... I love, treasure, adore and admire your shining presence in my life."[2] This romantically effusive dedication was entirely in the tradition of dozens of other printed and spoken acknowledgments of Deborah's centrality in his personal and artistic life over the decades.

While Carlos has remained largely silent about his divorce, he increasingly became vocal about his intentions to move into new musical directions. As early as his interview with Steve Heilig in 2000, Carlos had expressed an intense interest in working with Bill Laswell. One reason was Laswell's production of jazz-heavy metal guitarist Sonny Sharrock's best-sounding album, *Ask the Ages*, a recording putting Sharrock in the company of other jazz masters Carlos favored, saxophonist Pharoah Sanders and drummer Elvin Jones, both colleagues of yet another musical hero, John Coltrane. Sharrock shared with Carlos the desire to translate some of Coltrane's saxophone sound to electric guitar, am ambitious and arduous goal. Coltrane's music evolved into atonality, speech-like effects like screaming, shouting, and moaning, all of which risked sounding like noise when transferred to electric guitar. Coltrane's saxophone playing could be fashioned in close correspondence to his breathing patterns and embouchure, creating sounds like a human voice in the throes of ecstasy. This vocalizing has been difficult to achieve on electric guitar, in spite of myriad electronic processors that can make a guitar sounds like anything but a conventional guitar. The dominant tone that Carlos has achieved in a Coltrane vein is a rapturous, half-spoken, half-sung tone, an effect well achieved by Sharrock before his untimely death.

And there was a more direct tie to Carlos than the Sharrock connection. Laswell had creatively remixed two earlier albums by Carlos, *Love Devotion Surrender* and *Illuminations*. Laswell might have come to Carlos's attention because earlier in the 1990s Laswell released two remixes of two key musical ancestors Carlos admired: Bob Marley and Miles Davis. The Laswell remixes of these intensely spiritual recordings that matched Carlos with guitarist John McLaughlin and keyboardist/harpist

Alice Coltrane were released in 2001 under the title *Divine Light: Reconstructions & Mix Translations*. Laswell's "translation" involved adding depth through selective reverb and heightening the dominance of bass and keyboard in his remix. Essentially, Laswell created the illusion of a cosmically huge bass and organ soundscape that was rained upon by electric guitar notes furiously executed by Carlos. The album was released with Carlos Santana's name writ large on the cover, but some music stores filed the disk under "Bill Laswell" on the grounds that the Laswell remix departed significantly enough from the original albums by Carlos as to warrant identification with the remixer.

According to a story in *Billboard*, Carlos was to team up with Laswell sometime in 2008 to do a three-CD set entitled "The Father, Son, and Holy Ghost." According to reporter Gary Graff, Carlos was planning the album as a mainly instrumental effort that would include keyboardist Chester "CT" Thompson and drummer Narada Michael Walden. Supplementing the basic trio would be guest artists including jazz saxophonists Pharoah Sanders, Wayne Shorter, and Kenny Garrett. As of 2009 the project has yet to materialize.[3]

So it appears that Carlos will be re-emphasizing his dedication to jazz and spirituality, the theme that so strongly dominated his early 1970s music, and one that has periodically resurfaced since. Yet his ongoing friendship with music company honcho Clive Davis suggests that Carlos will keep an eye on creating commercially mainstream, chart-topping music. Whatever new directions he will assume, now as a bachelor and elder statesman of the rock 'n' roll revolution, he has solidly established an enduring place for himself in the history of popular world music. He also established with overwhelming force the centrality of the Latin music contribution within mainstream American popular music, making it possible for more Hispanic young people to believe that they may reach stardom by "rocking in the U.S.A."

And finally, through a lifetime of performing for humanitarian causes with a zeal and level of ongoing commitment unmatched by any major rock performer, Carlos has shown his fans how musical passion can be an instrument for bettering the world, albeit for the most part through causes identified with the American political Left. When rock 'n' roll was first broadcast on U.S. radio, some condemned it as "the devil's music," an accusation earlier aimed by some religious fundamentalists at the blues. The story of Carlos Santana has been one that reconnects us with rock music inspired by the voices of angels.

There are dangers associated with popular entertainers stepping beyond that role and transitioning into spokespeople for political and religious persuasions. Carlos has admitted to a number of interviewers how his political and spiritual allegiances have made him the target of various critics. Carlos responded to journalist Phil Sutcliffe's comment that some people thought Carlos was a crackpot for hearing angels direct his musical career: "There's a TV milk commercial now featuring an aging rock star who has an angel appear to him—of course it's me! (laughs)." Carlos once believed that Frank Zappa titled an album of Zappa guitar solos, *Shut Up 'N Play Yer Guitar*, specifically as an order aimed at Carlos. In support of that speculation, Zappa's album did have a tune entitled "Variations on the Carlos Santana Secret Chord Progression."

Rock entertainers have always had a push-pull with issues of respectability in the public eye, not unlike jazz and blues musicians before them. Remember that Bill Graham, the first serious business manager Carlos ever worked with, sought to portray the Santana band as a raw assortment of streetwise kids, forerunners of punk rockers. When the first incarnation of the Santana band dissolved after the recording of *Santana III*, Carlos began to shape an individual public image infused with mystical devotion and charitable service, a public image less saturated with streetwise recreational drug use and legally uncommitted sexual expression. And part of his benefit concerts have benefited humanitarian causes identified with the political Left, though hardly its radically revolutionary wing. It was daring for Carlos, as a major sixties rock star, to bring *any* hint of strong political allegiance into his music. His willingness to even indirectly espouse his political beliefs occurred in a nonconducive atmosphere.

Since rock stars have been often portrayed as "larger than life" celebrities, literally, since rock concerts regularly project gargantuan images of themselves during concerts, there is the danger of them taking themselves and their pronouncements too seriously. Much as millions of young people regularly buy products endorsed by rock stars, so they also can be impressed by belief systems presented like products and subject to the same faddism.

Yet something of Carlos's streetwise persona has remained. And it was a picture of Che Guevara, the doctor turned revolutionary in the strategic military service of Fidel Castro's Marxism, that brought it into public visibility. In what might be seen as a tempest in a teapot controversy from the perspective of non-Cubans unfamiliar with Cuban history, Carlos found himself at the center of a heated and protracted controversy in 2005. He appeared at the 77th Academy Award ceremony wearing a Che Guevara t-shirt and a crucifix pendant under a sport coat. His outfit was linked to the duet he performed by the actor and singer Antonio Banderas, star of the Oscar-nominated film, *The Motorcycle Diaries*. Banderas and Carlos performed a song from the film soundtrack, "Al Otro Lado Del Rio" (On the Other Side of the River), which was nominated for Best Original Soundtrack Music. The song's composer, Uruguayan singer/songwriter Jorge Drexler, was stopped by the show's producers from singing his own song, which was awarded the Oscar, on the grounds that the song's performance by the popular actor Banderas would ensure a larger viewer audience.

Understanding the meaning of Carlos's attire at the Academy Awards ceremony involves comprehending controversies surrounding Che Guevara, who has remained a highly loved, and despised, figure since his assassination by Bolivian militiamen in 1967. Through an internationally famous and commercially widely copied 1960 portrait of Che by photographer Alberto Korda, Che's image has also been one of the most successful marketing images of all time, featured on products ranging from bikinis to cigarette lighters. As author Patrick Symmes, author of *Chasing Che: A Motorcycle Journey in Search of the Guevara Legend*, wrote:

> His image has been appropriated for political, economic, and even spiritual purposes ...; his face is used to sell beer and skis, yet an English church group recently issued posters of Jesus Christ himself recast as Che. The affluent youth of Europe and North America have resurrected Che as an easy emblem of meaningless and unthreatening rebellion, a queer blending of educated violence and disheveled nobility, like Gandhi with a gun.[4]

At the Academy Award ceremony, Carlos framed the Korda iconic photo of Che emphasizing his Christ-like look by wearing a cross over the Che image. Yet the song Carlos performed with Banderas from *The Motorcycle Diaries* was a soundtrack to a film saga about the *pre-* Communist revolutionary Che, a romantic young man on the road to discovering his true mission in life: violently opposing peasant exploitation through violent revolutionary activity. The Che of the film was not anyone's Christ-like image. Yet the Korda photograph on Carlos's chest with a crucifix added, which Carlos proudly revealed to press photographers at the Academy Awards by pulling his sport coat away to clearly reveal the t-shirt and crucifix, sent at best an ambiguous message to his audience.

The esteemed jazz musician Paquito D'Rivera, an exile from Castro's Cuba, sent a widely published "Open Letter to Carlos Santana" that criticized Carlos for not realizing that Santana's music was banned in the Cuba run by Fidel Castro and Che Guevara, and that, far more important, Che was directly responsible for thousands of Cubans being imprisoned and executed without trial. One of those imprisoned but spared execution was D'Rivera's cousin Bebo, who was jailed as an alleged Christian counterrevolutionary. D'Rivera particularly focused on the crucifix Carlos wore: "The guerrilla guy with the beret with the star is something more than that ridiculous film about a motorcycle trip, my illustrious colleague, and to juxtapose Christ with Che Guevara is like entering a synagogue with a swastika hanging from your neck."[5]

Carlos, through his press representative, released this statement in response to his televised Academy Awards appearance:

> The image was not intended to project a single note of the hatred, anger or revolutionary ruthlessness displayed when Che Guevara was a revolutionary leader in Cuba. It was worn to honor the soulful young man portrayed in the movie, who awoke to the struggle of the disenfranchised and who had a profound political epiphany during a journey across South America. The image was not meant to be an endorsement about a man who helped to establish the Castro dictatorship in Cuba.

Santana's Cuban exile critics were unsatisfied with this statement and went on the attack through numerous Internet postings, accusing Carlos of being insensitive to the plight of Cuban exiles who fled their country after the Castro revolution, while employing them in his band, citing Armando Peraza as one famous example. The controversy continued with Carlos's guest appearance on Cuban American diva Gloria Estefan's 90 Millas album. Estefan and her producer-husband Emilio had long been known in their Miami community as strongly anti-Castro, not a surprising position since Estefan's father was a bodyguard for the disposed dictator Batista, whom Castro, with Che's help, overthrew.

When Estefan's album appeared in 2007, with a sticker on the front heralding Carlos's guest appearance, anti-Castro activists were quick to post photos from the Academy Awards and accused the Estefans of insensitivity to the pain of Cuban exiles, causing the Estefans to issue a press release stating:

Perhaps some people saw his [Carlos's] performance and his wardrobe and not what he expressed afterwards with respect to the matter. Mr. Santana spoke decisively during the interviews that were conducted for the documentary that will accompany our new project "90 Millas" and he expressed his desire to perform in a free Cuba.[6]

Yet another layer of complexity to the controversy can be spotted when viewing Internet posts accusing Carlos, whom his accusers variously identified as "Tijuanian" and "Mexican," as unfairly appropriating Cuban music. One Cuban American exile faulted Carlos for not playing the music of his own people, a critique that bizarrely resonated with the stinging comment jazz bassist Reggie Workman made to Carlos during the studio session for the collaborative album with Alice Coltrane, *Illuminations*.

Yet critics demanding that Carlos adhere to his Mexican musical heritage have ignored how much the music of Mexico has been interpenetrated by European and African influences over the centuries. Such critics have ignored the fact that pollination of musical styles across national borders has been accelerating since the Middle Ages, as musicians have discovered through their travels a wealth of new ideas.

From his beginnings in music in Mexico, Carlos has identified his musical focus as international in scope. He has never wavered from that international focus, though Afro-Cuban rhythms have been central to his music since the release of the first Santana album in 1969. In a sense, Carlos has translated everything from a Brahms melody ("Love of My Life" from *Supernatural*) to contemporary Senegalese tunes via the band Touré Kunda into a style where Afro-Cuban rhythms work as meaningful rhythmic foundation. Since he only arrived at the awareness of Afro-Cuban dance music after apprenticing himself to the blues, Carlos has had a somewhat abstract and stylized relationship to Afro-Cuban music, a music he first discovered through recordings rather than from seeing live concerts, showcasing Latin dances like the mambo and cha-cha.

This distance in his youth from the Latin music scene in Miami and New York helped Carlos feel free to fashion his own mutation of the Latin dance form. Latin music was simply one more musical orthodoxy, like the blues, which Carlos improvised upon despite the cries of some critics accusing him of producing ersatz Latin music. Since rock 'n' roll has been a fairly recent musical invention, most rockers haven't undergone complaints about inauthenticity or crass musical appropriation the way that many blues and jazz artists have undergone since the early twentieth century. But because he pushed the envelope of rock 'n' roll across styles and culture, making it more literate and sophisticated intellectually, Carlos has had to face those charges.

Yet his worldwide audience seems indifferent to the issue of how "pure" his music has been. It matters more to his millions of fans that it comes from Carlos's heart, and that implicitly cross-syncopating with his Afro-Cuban rhythms is the universal beat of the heart. While the term "globalization" has chiefly been used in reference to political and economic erosion of firm boundaries among nations, it has value as a term describing the music Carlos has forged. Long before music stores categorized albums as "world music," Carlos had transformed rock into a type of musical *lingua franca*, a common language based on energizing rocking rhythms, wailing and soaring electric guitar, and an adventure-some, improvisatory spirit. Such a generous style has involved compromises in order to reach a global audience. Long exchanges among percussionists found in salsa have been often eliminated from studio recordings, as have extended brass choruses. Lyrics have been nearly entirely in English, and very simple English, in order to maintain global appeal. But Santana's sense of "authenticity" has meant being authentic to his widely eclectic impulses. By doing so he has made himself comfortable as a world citizen with his individual style as his passport. As Carlos informed interviewer Steve Heilig, "I don't consider myself a Mexican who has to sell Mexico to everyone. I don't think Bob Marley felt he had to sell Jamaica. I think he saw himself as a planetary citizen. That's how I like to see myself."[7]

A major way Carlos has navigated a career path through the complex challenge of acting as a planetary citizen is through an emphasis on spontaneity in his music over rigid planning. Spontaneous behavior allowed more for adapting to a rapidly changing world, a point of view Carlos shared with a number of countercultural artists rising to fame in the 1960s. American studies professor Daniel Belgrad has identified this trend in American art sharply in his book *The Culture of Spontaneity: Improvisation and the Arts in Postwar America*.[8] A large number of interviews with Carlos over the years find him using the vocabulary of "the energy field," a term Belgrad identified as essential to American countercultural expression. In an interview with music journalist Michael Molenda, Carlos describes the summoning of musical energy through contacting his heart: "How fast can you get to your heart and not let anything get in the way—children, the rent, the set list, taxes, nothing? How fast can you get to that place in your heart where you don't even have to think about what to play, because the notes will play themselves. Those are the best notes."[9]

This is a statement reflecting the mystical side of Carlos that has always desired to escape mundane constraints. Since this interview was conducted a year after his divorce and with his children grown, the idea that "children" need not to get in the way of a perfectly sculpted guitar solo from the heart sounds poignant. Carlos's comment reflects an idealized romanticism about musical creativity that has existed side-by-side with a commitment for commercial success. The world of commercial success in pop music has never been strictly an affair of "the heart," as Bill Graham and Clive Davis often reminded Carlos. Yet the way Carlos has tirelessly given much of his accumulated fortune to charity has been perhaps a way to live with his contradictory impulses artistically, his rock-jazz forays another. The great mystic of American literature Walt Whitman wrote, "Do I contradict myself? Very well then I contradict myself. (I am large, I contain multitudes.)"[10]

Carlos is a personality with that same capacity that Whitman possessed to identify with the largest imaginable global audience. Such a total identification necessarily entails musical compromises. Rock, not jazz, is the *lingua franca* of international youth. So is rap. So are pop melodies that sound peppy and memorable through cheap speakers or earphones in vehicles and cars or through iPods. Carlos believes he can help change the world through the better by creating world music. Call it naive or simplistic if you wish. But only a tough cynic would question the sincerity, energy, and versatile musical talent he has brought to the challenges.

NOTES

1. "Carlos Santana, Wife Getting Divorced," Yahoo News, http://news.yahoo.com/s/ap/20071102/ap_en_ce/people_santana.

2. Santana, *Multi-Dimensional Warrior* (Columbia/Arista/Legacy 88697 102042).

3. Gary Graff, "Santana in a Trio Mood for Next Album," *Billboard*, November 28, 2007, http://www.billboard.com/bbcom/news/article_display.jsp?vnu_content_id=1003678509.

4. Quoted in book review of Patrick Symmes, *Chasing Che: A Motorcycle Journey in Search of the Guevara Legend* in *Outside*, February 2000, http://outside.away.com/outside/magazine/200002/200002review6.html.

5. Paquito D'Rivera, "Open Letter to Carlos Santana," March 25, 2005, Latin American Studies, http://www.latinamericanstudies.org/che/oscars.htm.

6. Cuban American Pundits, http://cubanamericanpundits.blogspot.com/2007/03/when-damage-cont.

7. Steve Heilig, "The World of Carlos Santana," *The Beat* 19, no. 1 (2000): 73.

8. Daniel Belgrade, *The Culture of Spontaneity: Improvisation and the Arts in Postwar America* (Chicago: University of Chicago Press, 1999). See chapter 1 for an overview of this subject.

9. Michael Molenda, "Multi-Dimensional Miracles: Carlos Santana Celebrates the Power of Intangibles," *Guitar Player*, December 2008, 100.

10. Walt Whitman, *Song of Myself*, sec. 51.

Chapter 8

CARLOS SANTANA AS A
SIXTIES "SURVIVOR"

A survey of the life and music of Carlos Santana would not be complete without placing the Santana story within the context of the 1960s. Perhaps no decade in the past century has been so much the object of spoken and written controversy. Two quotes about the era on the website of a contemporary political commentary, Sam Smith, seems particularly useful in reflecting on Carlos as an exemplification of the values and ideals of the 1960s:

> Sure, we were young. We were arrogant. We were ridiculous. There were excesses. We were brash. We were foolish. We had factional fights. But we were right.
>
> —Abbie Hoffman

> The accused have never denied the charge of misusing the funds of the student union. Indeed, they openly admit to having made the union pay some $1500 for the printing and distribution of 10,000 pamphlets, not to mention the cost of other literature inspired by Internationale Situationniste. These publications express ideas and aspirations which, to put it mildly, have nothing to do with the aims of a student union. One has only to read what the accused have written, for it is obvious that these five students, scarcely more than adolescents, lacking all experience of real life, their minds

confused by ill-digested philosophical, social, political and economic theories, and perplexed by the drab monotony of their everyday life, make the empty, arrogant, and pathetic claim to pass definitive judgments, sinking to outright abuse, on their fellow-students, their teachers, God, religion, the clergy, the governments and political systems of the whole world. Rejecting all morality and restraint, these cynics do not hesitate to commend theft, the destruction of scholarship, the abolition of work, total subversion, and a worldwide proletarian revolution with "unlicensed pleasure" as its only goal. In view of their basically anarchist character, these theories and propaganda are eminently noxious. Their wide diffusion in both student circles and among the general public, by the local, national and foreign press, are a threat to the morality, the studies, the reputation and thus the very future of the students of the University of Strasbourg.

> —1966 judgment in the case of students at the
> University of Strasbourg, members of the avant
> garde of what would become known around the
> world as the youth movement of the 1960s[1]

Both the laudatory quote by Abbie Hoffman and the accusatory statement by a German judge emphasize the extraordinary power of youthful energy to change the world. In the first instance, Abbie Hoffman, a political leader on the political Left in the United States, believed that the politically engaged of the sixties generation should take credit for promoting the victory of the civil rights movement and the end of the Vietnam War. In words echoing the sentiments of U.S. conservatives today, the Strasbourg judge implied that the leaders of the sixties should be credited with instigating ruinous anarchy, fostering a wholesale disrespect for political and religious authority, and attacking of the work ethic in favor of sheer hedonism.

How can we examine the life and music of Carlos Santana in light of these two diametrically opposite views of the era when Carlos came of age? While in the earlier chapters of this book a chronological examination of the Carlos Santana story has unfolded, in this final chapter the story of Carlos Santana is presented in terms of the decade that most shaped his character formation for life, the 1960s. These are the key ideas of the sixties that Carlos reformulated over the decades since.

ROCK MUSIC OPENED THE DOOR TO POLITICAL ACTIVISM

The words and music of Carlos Santana did not explicitly mention any political ideas until the 1980s. But Carlos made clear his political statement from the first year of his professional career on through benefit concerts for causes he believed in. Interestingly, this has been directed more to groups than to individuals. For example, his activities protesting the wars in Vietnam and Iraq have been more for organizations promoting peace than for individual politicians running on antiwar platforms. That distrust of politicians, Republican or Democratic, reflects a common trait of the baby boom generation. Carlos, like many of his sixties contemporaries in the rock star pantheon such as John Lennon and Jimi Hendrix, believed in the power of music to alter society in a more just direction. By donating a generous portion of his profits to causes he believed in, Carlos escaped the stigma attached to many rock celebrities of "selling out" to the establishment while profiting from music that supposedly was rebellious.

The extent of the charity work Carlos has done is well documented on the "Look to the Stars: The World of Celebrity Giving" website.[2] The causes listed by the site that Carlos has actively supported include Abuse, AIDS, At-Risk/Disadvantaged Youths, Children, Creative Arts, Education, Health, Human Rights, Hunger, Literacy, Voter Education, and Women. Linking these areas for charity has been a sixties sensibility Carlos embodied by emphasizing the welfare of those many politicians pretend are "out of sight," but for Carlos not "out of mind." The sixties were a time of political mobilization for groups perceived as "underdogs," in some cases, to use the haunting memoir title by jazz bassist Charles Mingus, those *Beneath the Underdog*. Another term for "underdog" is *marginalized*, and Carlos has worked to bring the needs of those on the margins of American society into plain view, front and center.

MAKING THE PLEASURE PRINCIPLE A MUSICAL LIFESTYLE

The sixties pop-music scene associated hit music with a hedonistic lifestyle more than any music up to that decade. While the recreational, and often self-destructive, use of alcohol and drugs had been commonplace among blues and jazz musicians at the start of the century, the mass media of the sixties romanticized and propagated a

highly sensationalized, romanticized view of such activities. The same
was true of sexual expression outside of the boundaries of conventional
marriage. The filmed documentary of the Woodstock Music Festival
emphasized a new sense of freedom of sexual expression, demonstrated
by an acceptance of public nudity in a music festival context. Also the
presence of female "groupies," young women after the sexual favors of
rock stars, was a part of the sixties rock scene in general. Carlos left
that "free love" scene behind when he became a committed spouse and
parent in the 1970s, but has continued to speak of his musical style
using imagery and phrases from the "free love" sixties scene.[3]

ROCK MUSIC SUGGESTED THAT UTOPIA WAS REALIZABLE IN OUR TIME

Carlos in 2008 told interviewer Phil Sutcliffe, "People say Woodstock
was useless, but I saw a collective adventure representing something that
still holds true today. When the Berlin wall came down, Woodstock was
in there, when Mandela was liberated Woodstock was in there, when
the world celebrated the year 2000 Woodstock was in there."[4] While
Carlos also told Sutcliffe that Altamont, the violent counterpoint to
Woodstock, was also "every day," Carlos's overwhelming philosophy
through the decades has been one of cosmic optimism, a belief that
powerful rock music can strike a resonant chord with the best in human
nature, crossing conventional religious and national boundaries. As
Carlos informed interviewer Michael Molenda, "God could not care less
if you call him Buddha, Allah, Jesus, or Krishna. The best part of you—
that's what God is, and it is in all of us. It's called the spark of the
divine."[5] Following that often reiterated credo of pan-spirituality, Carlos
then gave Molenda examples of solos by John Coltrane and Jimi Hendrix that touched that divine spark in everyone who heard them.

THE SIXTIES REACTIVATED AS 21ST-CENTURY SOCIAL NETWORKING BLOG

Nothing so poignantly brings into relief how Carlos has been a sixties
survivor than his social networking blog called "Architects of a New
Dawn."[6] It is described in the following fashion on its opening page:

> Architects of a New Dawn is a project, born from the dream
> and vision of Carlos Santana, to create a new global network

driven by extraordinary music and powerful media content. It is designed to engage people from all walks of life to work together to create positive change in the global community where love can replace fear and where peace can reduce conflict.

The name of the blog conjures up fascinating sources of inspiration. The "New Dawn" could suggest to someone knowledgeable about the history of occultism the famous "Hermetic Order of the Golden Dawn," a late 19th/early 20th–century mystical organization that included artists like the poet W. B. Yeats among its members. A less esoteric evocation that might have inspired Carlos was the title of the final album Jimi Hendrix had worked on before his tragic death, *First Rays of a New Rising Sun*. The use of "architect" was original with Carlos, but occurred during an era when architects were highly visible in pop culture as celebrities.

Also on the site's opening page is a statement from Carlos suggesting that this is the ripe moment in history to engage people to make a better world through global networking through the Internet. The sixties flavor of the blog can be discerned by going to the members section where member photographs favor baby boomers, so much so that one 20-something member of the blog community wonders why there aren't more members his age involved.

In a section of the site labeled "Solutions," 41 links are offered that might further elucidate the appeal of "Architects of a New Dawn." These include some traditionally and widely respected organizations as Amnesty International and Doctors Without Borders to a number of controversial websites by New Age healers and gurus, including the Chopra Center, Caroline Myss, and Jerry Jampolsky and Diane Cirincione. In a carefully worded preface to these links, the following statement is attached:

> We do not necessarily agree with all the actions, methods, or ideologies of each of these organizations. This page is not intended as an endorsement for membership in these organizations. It is simply a listing and a link to several of the organizations we support.

As was the case with the Che t-shirt controversy, Carlos seemed to have sent, through his press representations and legal council, an ambiguous message. Which organizations on this list has he supported wholeheartedly? How did he partially support, or not support, those whose actions, methods, or ideologies he didn't necessarily agree with? The hand of experienced legal counsel was reflected in this wording, an implicit recognition that the values of a sixties survivor like Carlos were still seen as controversial by many 21st-century Americans too young to even recall the sixties. An analogy would be the wording of herbal medicines, also favored by many sixties survivors, who regularly use them and believe in their efficacy, though the U.S. Food and Drug Administration compels labeling that reads next to herbal medicine claims, "This product is not intended to diagnose, treat, cure, or prevent any disease."

This ambiguity was perhaps part of Carlos being a sixties survivor. Questions about the deep rationale for his thinking, part of a conventionally rational analysis of human personality and motivation, come from as different state of mind than was common in the counterculture of the sixties. Carlos was a teenager in a Bay Area culture that gave enormous meaning to the irrational, intuitive, and mystical facets of personality and motivation. So he has been accused by his critics of espousing cosmically colored generalizations.

But to be fair, Carlos has dedicated his life to musical expression that synthesized an enormous amount of mystical and intuitive content. And even the staunchest defenders of a rationality-first philosophy of human nature have become stymied when trying to explicate musical creativity as a purely rational behavior. The New Age movement, largely populated by sixties survivors who used psychedelic drugs as Carlos did during that period, believed that their drug-induced visions encapsulated certain cosmic truths not yet discovered by science. When Carlos wrote lyrics praising the glories of "light," his use of the word harks back to Judeo-Christian mysticism, the countercultural worlds of alchemy, astrology, and kaballah, not the concept of light scientifically identified with Michael Faraday and Thomas Edison. As Carlos told interviewer Thor Christensen in talking about his music and comparing going to a rock concert to going to a church: "It's like church, but it's not plastic.... A lot of churches are like going to a very slick car dealer. But this church doesn't want your money—it wants you to invest in the light inside of you."[7] Christensen comments,

> Talk to Mr. Santana for very long and the word light pops up a dozen times. In the '70s, he briefly renamed himself Devadip Santana, a name his Indian guru Sri Chinmoy told him meant the light of the world. Inner light is also the

theme of *Multi-Dimensional Warrior*, a two-disc compilation of lesser-known songs from 1970–2002.

DEVELOPING "HIP CAPITALISM"

The development of the "Carlos" line of women's shoes has offered an example of what many sociologists have identified as "hip capitalism." As explained by Thomas Frank in *The Conquest of Cool: Business Culture, Counterculture, and the Rise of Hip Consumerism*:

> Rebel youth culture remains the cultural mode of the corporate moment, used to promote not only specific products but the general idea of life in the cyber-revolution. Commercial fantasies of rebellion, liberation, and outright "revolution" against the stultifying demands of mass society are commonplace to the point of invisibility in advertising, movies, and television programming.[8]

The "Carlos" shoe line advertising uses a language not unlike that used in the advertisements of "Fruitopia" by Coca-Cola (evocative of a ride on novelist and dramatist Ken Kesey's countercultural bus to personal freedom), Nike's shoe ad using the song "Revolution" by the Beatles, and Microsoft ("Where would you like to go today?," a question once used for far different reasons by dealers of psychedelic drugs). Here are some examples of shoe descriptions from the Carlos Shoe website. The shoes are described as communicating "the same passion and energy as Carlos Santana's music." Women are encouraged to "plot their moves" in the "Carlos by Carlos Santana 'Conspire' Wedge" that uses a python snake–textured upper. In part of the website showcasing a video of an ad for Santana shoes by Macy's, Carlos is playing various guitar runs to demonstrate how, in the guitarist's words, "Shoes are like women. They inspire beautiful music." Humorously concluding the ad, Donald J. Trump in another corner of a Macy's department store with his custom line of men's neckties claims, "My ties are beautiful. They don't need music."[9]

The Carlos Shoes were a joint venture of Deborah and Carlos Santana. It should be noted that a portion of the profits from the shoes goes to their nonprofit Milagro Foundation for underserved children internationally. That supports the notion that Carlos has carried the altruistic drive to make a more just world into the 21st century. But remaining ambiguous is a message from advertising for the shoes that might or might not have had Carlos's approval:

> Carlos Santana is more than a name for a brand. Although Carlos does not design the footwear himself, he is part of the design process. The interpretation of the multi-cultural, colorful imagery that surrounds Santana's music brings the shoes to life.[10]

An interesting contrast to the role Carlos had in creating his shoe line would be to consider how Jerry Garcia, the leader of the San Francisco psychedelic jam-band the Grateful Dead, developed his product line of men's ties. Garcia was enrolled as a serious student in the visual arts program at the San Francisco Art Institute and continued oil painting and watercolor painting throughout his life. This is not to suggest which form of hip capitalism is superior. It simply shows that the extramusical business activity Carlos's contemporary worked with was integral to a lifetime pursuit. One can only fantasize how the Macy's ad for Santana shoes would have concluded if Jerry Garcia was still alive to say, "My ties are as musical as your shoes."

RACIAL AND ETHNIC EQUALITY AS THE STANDARD FOR AN AMERICAN ROCK BAND

While racially mixed rock and pop bands are a commonplace in the 21st century, one need only look at pop music on television and on film from the early sixties to realize what a breakthrough the original lineup of the Santana band represented. The only other racially integrated bands that were featured at the Woodstock Music Festival in 1969 were Sly and the Family Stone and Jimi Hendrix's band. Carlos, having been subject to taunts in high school for being Mexican and speaking accented English, understood from that experience the alienation and injustice racial prejudice brought. Not only was a racially integrated rock band a novelty as late as the 1960s, but also high-profile blues bands and salsa bands tended, respectively, to consist of entirely African American members in the first case and Latin American musicians in the latter.

Carlos also overcame the anti-Semitism attached to Jewish musicians playing music outside of their ethnic roots by jamming with keyboardist Al Kooper and guitarist Michael Bloomfield. And he chose for his closest music business contacts Bill Graham and Clive Davis, both Jewish. If anti-Semitism seemed like less of an issue among musicians in the sixties, one would do well to recall the accusatory poetry and music criticism of that time by Amiri Baraka, then LeRoi Jones, who accused white people in general, and Jews in particular, of economically exploiting African American musicians.[11]

Carlos was always distrustful of labels attached to people and "walked his talk" when it came to personnel choices.

ELEVATING THE IMPORTANCE OF THE FEMININE IDEAL

Not surprisingly, Carlos as the son of an errant and often absent father greatly elevated his image of the ideal woman. The importance of the spiritual manifestation of the ideal woman was evident when Carlos returned alone to Tijuana, Mexico, in 1962 after repeatedly complaining to his mother about living in San Francisco. Alone and homeless, Carlos went to a church where there was a shrine to the Virgin of Guadalupe, a dark-skinned form of the Virgin Mary venerated throughout much of Latin America. He prayed and asked for guidance and protection for himself and his family.[12]

His Mexican Catholic background, where women are sometimes stereotyped as either prostitutes or virgins, might have contributed to this tendency to concentrate on the angelic side of women. Carlos's increasing tendency to elevate the feminine as a spiritual ideal is evident in the evolution of his song lyrics. The first three Santana albums feature song lyrics essentially warning women to be on their best behavior around men, the most famous being "Evil Ways." By the release of the *Supernatural* album three decades later, songs like "Maria Maria" and "Smooth" have lyrics that reinforce this heavenly image of women.

While the tendency to elevate the feminine ideal can be suggested by his Mexican Catholicism, his mother, who thought her son Carlos special because of his light complexion, also played a particular role. As *Los Angeles Times* journalist Agustin Gurza notes, such a light complexion was "considered a blessing in Mexico's color-based society."[13] Carlos concluded his largely autobiographical album *Havana Moon* with a traditional Mexican song with which his father had serenaded his mother.

As evidence of how Carlos's view of the feminine ideal marks his identity as a sixties survivor, one can recall how pleased Carlos was by the way women danced to the rhythms of his band. As journalist Tina Butler noted:

> the imminent feminism of the later 60s was preceded by this consolidation of a new feminine ideal. The model embodied

a sense of movement, paralleling a culture in transition. Because of her location in a period in flux, the ideal is presented paradoxically in fashion photography of this era. An ironic and conflicted figure, the "Single Girl" at once represented "movement," and yet, her capacity to move was limited by the fact that her primary function was to signify the ideal of a period. "Both in appearance, waif-like and adolescent, and in goals, to be glamorous and adored by men (in the plural) while economically independent," the "Single Girl" proffered a new definition of femininity.[14]

Finally, a CD compilation of Santana's music released by Sony International in Europe (and rarely available elsewhere) entitled *Love Songs* offers 14 selections that show just how romantically Carlos has viewed women over the decades. The titles track the tendency: "Life Is a Lady," "I Love You Much Too Much," and "Daughter of the Night."

Recalling the album cover of *Abraxas* with a dark goddess figure astride a conga drum, the cover of *Supernatural*, adapted from a painting by Michael Rios entitled "Mumbo Jumbo," both reaffirms the *Abraxas* imagery and suggests a new twist. At the center of the Rios painting is a dark goddess—but she looks less fierce and foreboding than the *Abraxas* goddess. Her left hand holds a conga drum, a less aggressive relationship than sitting astride it. Her right hand holds a guitar neck. She is the symbolic goddess who bridges the melodic and feminine guitar and the percussive and aggressively masculine drums. However Carlos will evolve in the future, as a man as well as musician, will very much be the consequence of how he acts to reconcile both energies.

NOTES

    1. "Free Thoughts: Sam Smith's Favorite Quotes—The 60s," The Progressive Review, http://prorev.com/quotes.htm (accessed January 30, 2009).

    2. "Carlos Santana's Charity Work," Look to the Stars: The World of Celebrity Giving, n.d., http://www.looktothestars.org/celebrity/639-carlos-santana (accessed January 30, 2009).

    3. One among many examples is the interview with Phil Sutcliffe in the UK rock magazine *Mojo*, no. 180 (November 2008): 45–48. Also see p. 44 of Steve Heilig's interview in *The Beat* 19, no. 1 (2000).

    4. Interview with Sutcliffe in *Mojo*, 47.

    5. Michael Molenda, "Multi-Dimensional Miracles: Carlos Santana Celebrates the Power of Intangibles," *Guitar Player*, December 2008, 99.

6. Architects of a New Dawn, www.architectsofanewdawn.com.

7. Thor Christensen, "Music Is a Spiritual Undertaking for Carlos Santana," *Dallas News*, September 15, 2008, http://www.dallasnews.com/sharedcontent/dws/ent/stories/DN-santana_0915gl.ART.State.Edition1.26f6add.html (accessed January 30, 2009).

8. Thomas Frank, *The Conquest of Cool: Business Culture, Counterculture, and the Rise of Hip Consumerism* (Chicago: University of Chicago Press, 1998), 4.

9. All quotes and video downloaded from www.carlosshoes.com.

10. "CARLOS by Carlos Santana," Zappos, n.d., http://www.zappos.com/n/br/b/372/CARLOS%20by%20Carlos%20Santana.html.

11. The poem "Black Dada Nihilismus," recorded with the New York Art Quartet, is an example of Baraka's anti-Semitism set to music, available on ESP CD.

12. Steve Heilig, "Carlos Santana," *Whole Earth*, Summer 2000, 74.

13. "Santana: An Average Guy and His Angel," *Los Angeles Times*, November 3, 2002, retrieved from http://www.religionnewblog.com/1110.

14. Tina Butler, "The Counterfeit Body: Fashion Photography and the Deceptions of Femininity, Sexuality, Authenticity and Self in the 1950s, 60s and 70s," May 9, 2005, retrieved from http://news.mongabay.com/2005/0507d-tina_butler.html. Material in quotes is from Hilary Radner, "On the Move: Fashion Photography and the Single Girl in the 1960s," in *Fashion Cultures: Theories, Explorations and Analysis* (New York: Routledge, 2000), 128–42.

Chapter 9

CARLOS SPEAKS: INTERPRETATIONS AND REBOUNDING QUESTIONS

Carlos has been loquacious with reporters for decades, so much so that a small book could be comprised out of quotations. Because he has been so publicly outspoken about his life and music, it seems fitting to conclude with a number of his key quotations that were given "on the run." Quotations explained within lengthy and highly substantial interviews have been incorporated earlier in this book. But what about his hundreds of soundbites? They are suggestive—and in this chapter each will be followed by some plausible speculation about how they fit in the larger picture of Carlos as musician and celebrity.

> Some songs are just like tattoos for your brain ... you hear them and they're affixed to you.[1]

The image of the tattoo is telling. When Carlos began his musical career in the 1960s, tattoos were a body decoration chiefly identified with the lower classes in the United States, and often identified with blue-collar workers and ex-military men. For Carlos's fans who discovered him in 1999 through *Supernatural*, tattoos were thought of as hip and trendy for all ages and classes. But looking beyond the literal change in the ubiquity of tattoos across generations, the metaphor Carlos chose, songs equaling "tattoos for your brain," is telling. It reinforces the status of Carlos as a master of formulaic and "hooky" pop songs with highly memorable melodies. It would be more complex, if even possible, to have a jazz tune Carlos has recorded having that permanent imprint on a fan's brain since jazz entails complicated and lengthily developed melodic improvisations that are difficult to commit to long-term memory.

But the quote can also be interpreted as both a wish and a boast. Even the relatively simple pop songs on *Supernatural, Shaman,* and *All That I Am* might not necessarily fix themselves so indelibly on a music fan's synapses. Behind that boast might be a measure of wishful thinking on Carlos's part. Since a great deal of rock and pop music has proven ephemeral in the public's mind during the past fifty years, the reason why Carlos would hope his music has made a lasting mark is understandable.

> Music is the union of two lovers' melody and rhythm. The melody is the woman, and the rhythm is the man.

This quotation is actually from Hindu scripture attributed to an unknown author from thousands of years ago. It might have been appropriated by Sri Chinmoy, who often quoted Hindu scripture. Carlos might have heard it through that source. Nevertheless, the repeated comparison of music as a union of lovers has been an assertion Carlos has made to audiences for years, sometimes turning the quote so it suggests explicit sexual passion. The following quote demonstrates his slant:

> If our history can challenge the next wave of musicians to keep moving and changing, to keep spiritually hungry and horny, that's what it is all about.

The oracular, priestly sound of this and other authoritarian assertions Carlos has made about music and the meaning of life have caused some to question the reason for his outspokenness. Carlos has answered questions about the reasons for his outspokenness this way:

> That's a good question. I say it every day in interviews and when I'm on stage, and people say, how come he doesn't just play and be quiet? You have a Fox network that says celebrities shouldn't have opinions.

Outspokenness was one of Carlos's characteristics from his childhood on, when in no uncertain terms he offered his bristly opinions to his parents. He was emphatically assertive in telling his father how he wanted no part of the family's mariachi tradition. After he moved with his family to settle in San Francisco, he was blunt in informing his mother that life there was not satisfactory and he wanted to return to Mexico. That kind of outspokenness to his parents in his youth was unconventional for someone raised in rural Mexico. It marked the fact that Carlos as a youth took the artistic imperatives of his inner voices with great seriousness and urgency.

As he transitioned into the first stage of his professional music career, he was under the tutelage of Bill Graham, a combination artistic and business guru to Carlos. Graham was notorious, even in the context of the freewheeling countercultural scene, for loudly giving his opinions about sundry matters with great dramatic flair and emotional white heat. While Carlos has always been more soft-spoken and conciliatory in speech, he has carried on the Graham tradition of offering the press quotable, sometimes sensational, soundbites. Perhaps by eschewing what was Graham's bellicose delivery, Carlos has found a way to communicate his political and musical opinions in a genial and beguiling manner, avoiding the list of enemies that dogged Graham. When Carlos plays in support of global peace, his vocal tone has suggested that he has "walked his talk" This gentlemanly manner of expressing his opinions has been demonstrated when reporters asked Carlos about his feelings about his ex-wife Deborah. In an interview, UK music journalist Phil Sutcliffe asked if Carlos would talk about his terminated relationship. Carlos spoke candidly: "I chose not to because everything we did together until she decided she was done with me, it stands on its own. Beautiful, perfect, aesthetically, spiritually, momentarily. Our children alone ... She helped me along the way of self-discovery and hopefully I did the same thing with her."[2]

> Life, at least with us, doesn't need to fall like a military drill.
> The way we do things, we don't need windows and doors
> and ceilings. Things just happen when they happen.

This quotation illuminated part of Carlos's sixties identity in affirming an aesthetics based on spontaneity and improvisation. But it also indicates how he opposes pure spontaneity and unstructured thinking to his perception of the rigidity of military-style thinking. A middleground of working as a musician and person combining the best of both planning and spontaneity is not found in this quotation by Carlos, or any others easily found. Perhaps his dependence on the calculated business acumen of Bill Graham and Clive Davis has been a compensation for the freedom he has felt as an improvising musician operating with

minimal boundaries conceptually. His architectural metaphor is stimu-
lating. What does an architectural structure look like without windows,
doors, and a ceiling?

> We want to extend an invitation to healing.... Turn off
> CNN and turn on the light in your own heart.

As do a number of Santana's pithy quotations, this comment demonstrates an "either-or" choice. Either one is spiritually attuned every
day—or one is ensnarled by being excessively caught off in mundane
matters. "CNN" functions as a code word for the absolutely earthbound
in this comment, as "Fox Network" was a code word for conservative
television broadcasting in a previous quote. The emphasis on the thera-
peutic value of his music as a healing modality was exemplified in the
popular collaboration between Carlos and the blues great John Lee
Hooker on Hooker's album, *The Healer*. This album consisted not only
of the title-song collaboration, but collaborations with other noteworthy stars, including Robert Cray and Bonnie Raitt. One might consider
Hooker's *The Healer* his attempt to emulate the formula of Carlos's *Supernatural*. In over 70 albums prior to this 2001 release, Hooker often
performed boogie-woogie and had long showcased lyrics about completely mundane and even irreligious matters, as "Whiskey and
Women," the title of one popular Hooker song, indicates. On the
music video available on the Internet of Hooker and Carlos performing
"The Healer," Hooker's performances appear like a spoken and sung
stream of consciousness with only the core message that "Blues is a
healer all over the world."[3] The message seemed like more like
Carlos's.

> My role is to complement. It's nothing new. I've been doing
> this since 1968. I am very perceptive; I am a very secure per-
> son. So therefore, it's easy for me just to step back and
> complement.

The jockeying for leadership within the original Santana band in the
period between their first Columbia eponymously titled album and
Abraxas might call into question the complete accuracy of Carlos's
assertion of pleasure at complementing others. Carlos asserted leadership of the band at that time so strongly that the rest of the band went
on tour without him to assert their group identity. Similar debates
about Carlos's role as undisputed band leader also marked the studio

sessions for *Santana III* and *Caravanserai*. No one can contest the fact that Carlos has complemented recordings of dozens of major musicians through adding tasteful guitar solos. One might dispute whether his place in rock 'n' roll history was established chiefly by how he has complemented other musicians. Only the massive international popularity of *Supernatural* in 1999 seemed to solidify that facet of Carlos's identity.

> It's time for people to learn that we are all mixed up inside. That is why there is so much diversity on my records. I can relate to so many cultures and I want that to be reflected in my music.

Carlos discovered his cultural diversity internally while a youth in Mexico as he grew gradually aware that mariachi music didn't connect with him—but American blues did. Another leap in understanding his hybrid identity came during his first tour with his band in the West African nation of Ghana in 1971. That experience moved Carlos into a reckoning with the African roots of his music. The percussionists in his band throughout his career have hailed from Cuba and Puerto Rico, bringing yet another culture energy into his hybrid identity. Touring on every continent broadened Carlos's perspective cross-culturally over the years.

A word Carlos has favored in interviews with the press since 1999 has been "multidimensional." In an interview with a *Latin Beat* magazine reporter just after *Supernatural* was released he explained what "multidimensional" meant to him: "It is your choice if you just want to be a Chicano living around four blocks in the Mission [District] but that is not who you are completely. You and I are multidimensional spirits with tremendous opportunities and possibilities."[4]

That faith in a multidimensional Self with nearly unlimited opportunities and possibilities that Carlos heroically maintained has hardly been a belief commonly found in all cultures. It has been particularly uncommon in much of Eastern Europe, Asia, and Africa. It historically has been a quintessential American cultural belief, going as far back as America's founders who added the novel notion that every citizen should be entitled to "Life, liberty, and the pursuit of happiness." Thomas Jefferson, who penned that phrase, was likely influenced by the 17th-century English philosopher John Locke. Locke wrote about it in his essay "Concerning Human Understanding":

> The necessity of pursuing happiness [is] the foundation of liberty. As therefore the highest perfection of intellectual

nature lies in a careful and constant *pursuit of true and solid happiness*; so the care of ourselves, that we mistake not imaginary for real happiness, is the necessary foundation of our liberty.

Contemporary historian Carol V. Hamilton interpreted Locke's passage in this manner:

The Greek word for "happiness" is *eudaimonia*. In the passage above, Locke is invoking Greek and Roman ethics in which *eudaimonia* is linked to *aretê*, the Greek word for "virtue" or "excellence." In the *Nicomachean Ethics*, Aristotle wrote, "the happy man lives well and does well; for we have practically defined happiness as a sort of good life and good action." Happiness is not, he argued, equivalent to wealth, honor, or pleasure. It is an end in itself, not the means to an end. The philosophical lineage of happiness can be traced from Socrates, Plato, and Aristotle through the Stoics, Skeptics, and Epicureans.[5]

The life and musical career of Carlos Santana has been in pursuit of that true and solid happiness that comes beyond grasping for fame and fortune. At a time when so many Americans and citizens of the globe settle for a pursuit of happiness aligned to purely fame and fortune, Carlos Santana's words and music can serve as a reminder of happiness derived from an artistic and spiritual pursuit.

NOTES

1. All the Carlos Santana quotes in this chapter were retrieved from http://www.quotesdaddy.com/author/Carlos+Santana. They also appear on a dozen Internet sites created by fans of Carlos and the band.

2. Phil Sutcliffe, "Carlos Santana: The Mojo Interview," *Mojo*, no. 180 (November 2008): 48.

3. YouTube, http://www.youtube.com/watch?v=DXZ9DSrWgYw.

4. Louise Chipley Slavicek, *Carlos Santana* (New York: Chelsea House Publishers, 2006), 102.

5. Carol V. Hamilton, "The Surprising Origins and Meaning of the 'Pursuit of Happiness,'" January 28, 2007, History News Network, http://hnn.us/articles/46460.html.

SELECTED DISCOGRAPHY

The following dozen albums are highlights of Carlos Santana's career that includes nearly four dozen albums.

Abraxas. This album Carlos has identified as the "sentimental favorite" of all of his records. It captures the first popular version of the Santana band at their most musically cohesive. It also was the album that offered sonic clarity for the instrumentalists for the first time. The interplay between Carlos and keyboardist Gregg Rolie is best showcased here. The single from the album, "Black Magic Woman," became an international hit.

Santana III. The original band's swan song had a rigorous and unparalleled interplay between Carlos and sparing guitarist Neal Schon that brought out some of the finest solos in both men's careers.

Caravanserai. This was the first album where Carlos began his transition into fusing rock and jazz in a moody, atmospheric way. It also was primarily an album of instrumentals, a concept Carlos would later revisit.

Welcome. With a stellar cast of guest musicians that included vocalist Flora Purim, guitarist John McLaughlin, and vocalist Leon Thomas, this album was the most comprehensive jazzy album Carlos would ever record, and specifically reveals the impact of jazz legend John Coltrane on Carlos's playing.

Borboletta. A foray into light Brazilian pop with a rock-jazz undercurrent that might have reflected the influence of the jazz fusion group led by Chick Corea, Return to Forever. Original lyrics by Carlos reflect his involvement with Sri Chinmoy's spirituality.

Amigos. Could also be called *Abraxas Revisited.* A wholehearted return to Latin rock with minimal jazz elaboration. Perhaps the best showcase for the call-and-response between Carlos and keyboardist Tom Coster.

Moonflower. A seamless blend of live and studio recordings. Marked by the unlikely Latinized cover of "She's Not There," a crucial hit for the Zombies, a UK band of the 1960s.

Havana Moon. A musical autobiography in which Carlos's father offers a vocal on the same Mexican love song he performed decades earlier to the woman who would become his spouse for life. Texas blues-rock guitarist Jimmy Vaughan and Carlos duel effectively.

Blues for Salvador. The first Grammy Award for Carlos for "Best Rock Instrumental" is one of several dynamically dynamic guitar-driven instrumentals of this rock album with a strong jazz influence revealed in guitar solos in honor of jazz giants John Coltrane and Charles Mingus. The most tenderly lyrical side of Carlos's playing was showcased by "Bella," an instrumental dedicated to his daughter.

Dance of the Rainbow Serpent. Of the many compilations of Carlos's recordings, mainly for Columbia Records, this well-annotated and sequenced three-disc set is the finest and most comprehensive. Highpoints include selections from collaborations with John Lee Hooker, John McLaughlin, Vernon Reid, Weather Report, and the African drummer Olatunji.

Multi-Dimensional Warrior. An anthology that carefully cherrypicks the best songs and instrumentals on two discs from the 1980s on. It reframes the best moments of albums that met with limited public and press acceptance.

Supernatural. The album that launched Carlos's career as a 21st-century superstar who had changed with the times. Young hip-hop stars joined rock veterans like guitarist Eric Clapton for 13 radio-friendly tunes that sold 25 millions internationally and presented Carlos with eight Grammy awards.

SELECTED BIBLIOGRAPHY

BOOKS

Belgrade, Daniel. *The Culture of Spontaneity: Improvisation and the Arts in Postwar America*. Chicago: University of Chicago Press, 1999.

Christgau, Robert. *Rock Albums of the 70s: A Critical Guide*. New York: Da Capo Press, 1990.

Davis, Clive, with James Willwerth. *Clive: Inside the Record Business*. New York: William Morrow, 1975.

Experience Music Project/Science Fiction Museum and Hall of Fame. *American Sabor: Latinos in U.S. Popular Music*. Seattle: EMP and SFM, 2007.

Fernandez, Raul A. *Latin Jazz: The Perfect Combination*. San Francisco: Chronicle Books, 2002.

Fong-Torres, Ben. *Not Fade Away: A Backstage Pass to 20 Years of Rock and Roll*. San Francisco: Miller Freeman, 1999.

Frank, Thomas. *The Conquest of Cool: Business Culture, Counterculture, and the Rise of Hip Capitalism*. Chicago: University of Chicago Press, 1998.

Graham, Bill, and Robert Greenfield. *Bill Graham Presents My Life Inside Rock and Out*. New York: Da Capo Press, 2004.

Henderson, David. *'Scuse Me While I Kiss the Sky: Jimi Hendrix, Voodoo Child*. Updated ed. New York: Atria, 2008.

Lemke, Gayle, and Jacaeber Kastor. *The Art of the Fillmore: The Poster Series 1966–1971*. 2nd. ed. New York: Da Capo Press, 2005.

Leng, Simon. *Soul Sacrifice: The Santana Story*. London: Firefly Publishing, 2000.

McCarthy, Jim, with Ron Sansoe. *Voices of Latin Rock: The People and Events That Created the Sound.* Milwaukee: Hal Leonard Corporation, 2004.

Mingus, Charles. *Beneath the Underdog.* New York: Vintage, 1991.

Norman, Philip. *Sympathy for the Devil: The Rolling Stones Story.* New York: Simon and Schuster, 1984.

Oliver, Paul. *Screening the Blues.* New York: Da Capo Press, 1989.

Porter, Lewis. *John Coltrane: His Life and Music.* Ann Arbor: University of Michigan Press, 2000.

Roberts, John Storm. *The Latin Tinge: The Impact of Latin American Music on the United States.* New York: Oxford University Press, 1979.

Santana, Deborah. *Space Between the Stars: My Journey to an Open Heart.* New York: One World/Ballantine, 2006.

Shapiro, Marc. *Carlos Santana: Back on Top.* New York: St. Martin's Griffin, 2002.

Slavicek, Louise Chipley. *Carlos Santana.* New York: Chelsea House, 2006.

WEBSITES

www.santana.com

This is the only authorized music website of Carlos Santana and contains a wealth of information about recordings and tours.

www.milagrofoundation.org/default.asp

The Milagro Foundation created by Carlos Santana and his family in 1998 to promote educational opportunities for youth is explained in full.

www.architectsofanewdawn.com/vision

Carlos Santana created this social networking blog with an emphasis on New Age spirituality.

www.santana.com/sights/disc_complete.asp

The only authorized discography of all legal recordings of Carlos Santana, including solo and band recordings as well as guest appearances on albums by other artists, is available at this page of the official Santana site.

www.musicbox-online.com/santana.html

This is a page dedicated to Carlos Santana reviews (concerts and recordings) updated on "The Music Box," an e-zine of pop-music matters.

www.everyguitarist.com/carlos_santana.htm

Details about the guitars Carlos Santana currently favors can be found on this website.

www.leeconklin.com/

   The website of Lee Conklin, the poster artist whose design for the cover
   of the first Santana album, a visionary lion, is still widely reproduced
   and identified with the Santana band of 1969.

www.sfmuseum.org/hist1/rock.html

   A comprehensive chronology of the key events in San Francisco rock
   from 1965 to 1969 published by the Virtual Museum of the City of San
   Francisco.

www.woodstock69.com/index.htm

   A useful gathering of accounts and photographs from the Woodstock
   Music Festival that brought the Santana band to global attention.

www.markguerrero.net/misc_37.php

   A helpful overview of Latin rock by an influential Latin rock musician
   that offers a broad context for understanding Carlos Santana's music.

INDEX

About the Author

NORMAN WEINSTEIN is the author of *A Night in Tunisia: Imaginings of Africa in Jazz* (1992), *Gertrude Stein and the Literature of the Modern Consciousness* (1970), and six books of poetry, the most recent being *No Wrong Notes* (2005).